ESSENTIAL SURVIVAL GUIDE

POPULAR MECHANICS

ESSENTIAL SURVIVAL GUIDE

THE ONLY BOOK YOU NEED IN ANY EMERGENCY

HEARST
books

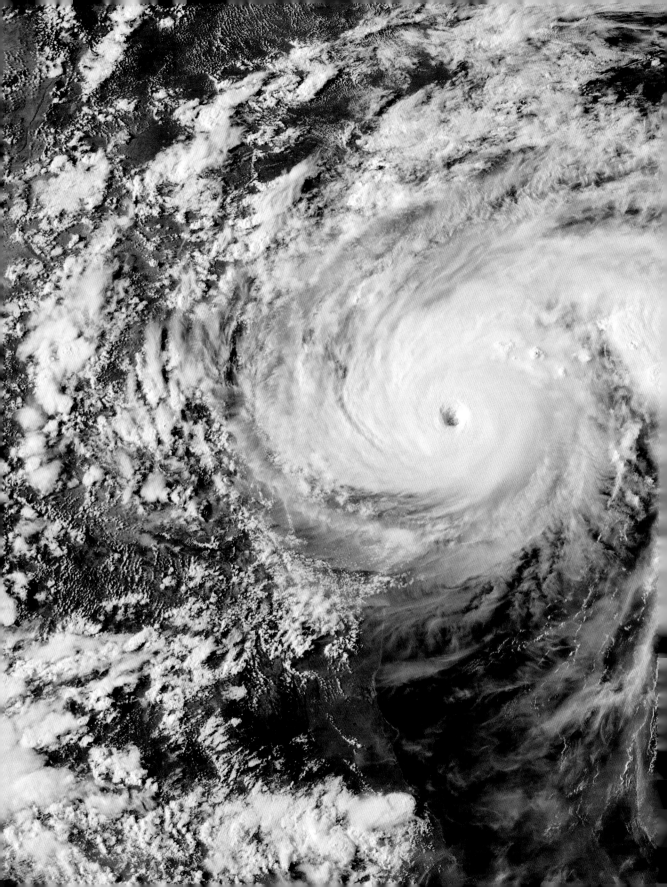

How to Survive

WHEN I WAS in fourth grade, my teacher suggested a book to read over the summer: *My Side of the Mountain*, the classic novel by Jean Craighead George about a teenage boy who runs away and ends up living in a hollowed-out tree and training a hawk. I never ran away from home, but I always wondered if I could have survived the way the boy in the book does.

Recently my wife and I read the book and showed the 1969 film version to our two boys. We asked them if they thought they could make it out in the wild—one said yes, the other wasn't so sure.

Survival means different things to different people in different situations. Throughout its existence, which spans 115 years and counting, *Popular Mechanics* has regularly published stories about all kinds of survival: in the woods alone; stuck in a mountain crag with no water; marooned on an iceberg as polar bears approach; trapped in a car by a fallen tree. Survival can mean simple self-sufficiency—living off the land, relying on only oneself for food, shelter, and water. It can mean digging a bunker in the backyard and stocking it with candles and Spam. Or there's my friend Eliot. The other day he found himself locked in his own bathroom in his apartment in New York City with no phone. After twenty minutes he was able to dismantle the entire door knob and lock using only a nail clipper.

Survival.

For this book, we've compiled our very best survival tactics, secrets, stories, firsthand advice, and gear recommendations in one place. The information in these pages was as relevant a century ago as it is now, when everything from climate conditions to global politics is rife with uncertainty. Keep it on the shelf in the basement next to your go bag, in the garage with your flares, or in the bunker out back. Study it. It contains not just knowledge about the most reliable waterproof fabrics but also wisdom on how to approach any situation in which survival is a question. Even if you're not the doomsday type, we all have in the back of our minds those three words that make a book like this indispensable: You never know.

Good luck out there.

RYAN D'AGOSTINO
Editor in Chief

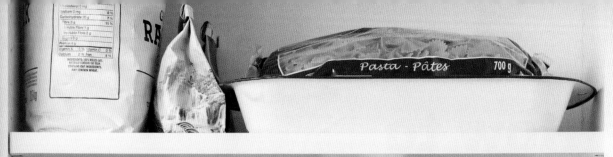

1.

Planning

LIFE IS GOOD. THE FAMILY IS HAPPY,
THE SKY IS CLEAR. THERE'S NO BETTER
TIME TO PREPARE.

Are You Prepared?

HURRICANES, FLOODS, WILDFIRES, TORNADOES—DISASTERS CAN TURN A REGION UPSIDE DOWN IN A DAY. AND FOR SOME UNLUCKY FAMILIES THE CRISIS MAY LAST FOR WEEKS, IF NOT MONTHS, UNTIL POWER AND CLEAN WATER SUPPLIES ARE RESTORED. SMART DISASTER PLANNING CAN HELP YOU THRIVE, NOT JUST SURVIVE, IN THE AFTERMATH.

ONE MONTH OF MREs and dehydrated meats and vegetables have their place, but you can maintain a comfortable stockpile of food without treating it like a culinary last resort. The strategy is called "store what you eat, eat what you store" and it means creating a rotating buffer of food that can be built up over time. Surprisingly, there's little consensus on how much of a buffer is necessary, but we suggest at least four weeks' supply. This photo shows 315,000 calories of food, plus the water needed to cook it—that's enough to keep a typical family of four fed for a month. It's a combination of carbs (rice, beans, pasta) and easy-to-eat canned goods (soup, fruit, veggies, tuna, peanut butter), as well as sanity savers such as chocolate and coffee. So hunker down and dig in.

LONG-TERM PLANNING

Disaster planning begins before you even choose your home, with a simple investigation of the risks that you will face. Is the house in a flood zone? Is there a history of hurricanes, wildfires, tornadoes? Then, once you're settled, you steadily build up resources, secure what's important to you, and turn your home into a survivable system. And when disaster hits, you'll be prepared.

FILL UP EVERY BASIN: FEMA suggests you store at least one gallon per person per day in the event of an emergency—28 gallons per week for a family of four. But that wasn't nearly enough for Conway Yee's family in Weston, Connecticut, after Hurricane Sandy knocked out power lines and disrupted his well-water supply for a week. To keep hydrated

and clean, "we went through 20 gallons a day" for drinking and washing, he says. They ended up driving to the local high school to refill their supply. "If a storm is approaching, I suggest you fill up every tub, sink, and water bottle in the house," says survival instructor and star of TV's *Dual Survival* Cody Lundin. A standard bathtub holds 109 gallons. Stuck with a stand-up shower? You can purchase 55-gallon plastic drums online for $70 and up.

SAVE YOUR BYTES: The best way to protect your data from a natural disaster is to back it up to a remote location. Mozy, one of several online backup solutions, will store 125 GB for $120 per year. (Dropbox and Google Drive give away a few gigabytes of storage for free.) If you'd rather store your data with someone you trust, buy two 2 TB network-attached storage drives and split them both into two equal partitions. Give one drive to a relative who lives in another state and then have the drives back up to each other over the Internet using rsync software. Both you and your relative will get local backup and a mirrored remote backup.

AquaPail 1000
Pour filthy water through the pail filter and clean, bacteria- and virus-free water drains out the bottom. No pretreatment is necessary. This model is good for up to 1,000 gallons.

BE FUEL SMART: Storing large amounts of gasoline to run your car and generator is dangerous and expensive. The gasoline must be treated with fuel stabilizer or used and replenished every few months. Instead, store six to 10 empty five-gallon cans and fill them at the gas station in the days before a storm. And don't forget propane for your outdoor grill. When utilities go down, the barbecue becomes your most reliable cooking tool.

A Brief Guide to Prepper Jargon

BOB: Bug-out bag

GENNY: Generator. Just say it.

HARDENED ELECTRONICS: Impervious to the effects of particle radiation or electromagnetic radiation

MAD: Mutually assured destruction, e.g., nuclear war

WROL: Without rule of law

YOYO: You're on your own. No relation to YOLO.

EDC: Everyday carry. Can be a phone or lighter or a knife or multitool.

BALLISTIC WAMPUM: A stockpile of ammunition that can be used for trade or as currency

GOBLIN: Someone who will start looting or committing other crimes in a survival situation

BIB: Bug-in bag. Everything you need to ride out an emergency at home.

MARAUDERS: People who collect guns rather than supplies. Their plan: to raid the prepared and eliminate the competition.

BUDDY BURNER: A homemade stove for cooking

DEEP LARDER: Long-term food storage

GOLDEN HORDE: The mass of helpless city dwellers who will pour out of metropolitan areas in an emergency

OPSEC: Operations security. Sharing your survival plans with other people is weak OPSEC.

BEYOND FIRST AID: A basic first-aid kit may not be enough to get you through the worst of a disaster. It's a good start—you do want bandages, gauze pads, aspirin, hydrocortisone, antiseptic wipes, etc.—but unexpected emergencies demand unconventional remedies. We asked Mykel Hawke, former Green Beret medic and host of *Elite Tactical Unit* on the Outdoor Channel, what he would add. His list: duct tape—great for wound closure, splints, and casts. Superglue—excellent for small, deep wounds. Use tape to hold while drying. Tampons—an unexpected tool for stanching heavy bleeding. Needle-nose pliers—use for removing large splinters or nails.

SAFE DEPOSIT DOCS: Keep copies of your insurance papers, household deed, and birth and marriage certificates in a safety deposit box. Also include a home video documenting your house. If your house gets destroyed, those documents are vital for reconstructing what you've lost.

NEAR-TERM PLANNING/ AFTERMATH

Within 72 hours, a storm can evolve from remote possibility to life-altering event. Most disasters give a bit of lead time—with a tornado, that's just long enough to get to the basement; with a hurricane, there's often enough warning for the unprepared to empty a whole region's supermarket shelves. But whether you've got minutes or days, use the time wisely. Focus on getting your family to a safe place and preparing for the cleanup.

FAST-TRACK SUPPLIES: In the days before Tropical Storm Irene, in 2011, Glenn Derene knew the storm was headed for his house on the Connecticut coast. He went to his computer and joined Amazon Prime. The service offers free two-day delivery on everything from generators to water to batteries. "A package full of goods arrived on my doorstep the morning before the storm," he says. "I spent my time preparing my home, not driving from store to store."

SECURE MISSILES: Go through the yard and tie down or bring inside anything that might go flying in high wind. That includes lawn furniture, wheelbarrows, garden tools, potted plants, and any construction materials.

CHARGE 'EM UP: Before the power goes down, plug in every rechargeable device you own and top off the batteries. After the lights go out, a simple DIY recharging station can replenish your laptops, cellphones, tablets, and power tools for days. Here's how it works: Before the storm, use a battery charger ❶, such as DieHard's micro-processor-controlled model, to charge up a gel-cell deepcycle battery ❷, such as the Optima BlueTop. After the local grid goes dark, unhook the battery and attach an inverter ❸, such as the Cobra 400-watt power inverter. Now sit back and enjoy some homemade juice.

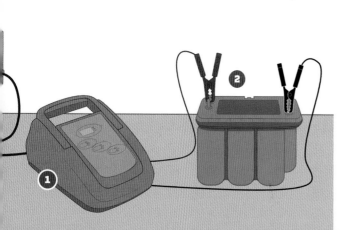

STRATEGY:
POWER

	POWER	FUEL	CAVEAT
 **STANDBY** ($1,800 to $5,000 with transfer switch)	Designed to feed into a household electrical system, small seven-kw units can power a few circuits; larger 20-plus-kw models can handle the whole house.	Standby generators typically run on natural gas or propane. Expect to use at least 140 cubic feet of natural gas per hour. At fall 2017 prices, that's about $1.44 every 60 minutes.	Double the cost for installation, plus more for yearly maintenance
 **LARGE PORTABLE** ($400 to $2,500)	These generators produce 3,000 to 10,000 watts and can either plug into a transfer switch or hook up to individual appliances through heavy-duty extension cords.	Gasoline consumption will range from eight to 20 gallons per day depending on the unit and what you're powering.	If you don't have 100-plus gallons of gasoline on-site, you'll be back in the gas line within days.
 **SMALL PORTABLE** ($900 to $1,150)	Compact and relatively lightweight (40 to 100 pounds), these generators produce between 800 and 3,500 watts and use an inverter to produce a clean power signal that won't harm sensitive electronics.	These units can run for up to nine hours on one gallon of gas, so if you run this generator judiciously, you can get a week's worth of use from 10 gallons.	Good for powering some lights, the fridge, and electronics— just not all at the same time.

ENTERTAIN YOURSELF: Riding out a disaster can take a surprisingly long time. Whether you stay at home or evacuate, plan out some activities that will keep kids busy and adults sane. Think board games, books, playing cards, puzzles, and a tablet stocked with video games and movies.

GET A POOL PUMP: If your basement regularly takes on water, an installed sump pump is the way to go. But if you don't have one and a storm surge is on the way, consider a gas-powered water pump. A 5.5-hp model can pump 150 gallons per minute out of a flooded basement and it works when the electricity is out. You can get one for under $250, or better yet, split the cost with your neighbors since they'll probably be affected by the surge, too. But don't pump out any basement unless you're sure the power's off and there's no sewage contamination.

BE LOCATION SAVVY: "It's really important to be geographically aware of where you live," says Greg Carbin, the warning-coordination meteorologist with the National Weather Service dealing with downed trees. Warnings for tornadoes and severe storms with hail are often geographically precise. So it's really useful to know what part of town you're in (northwest, city center) and your proximity to certain landmarks (town hall, a nearby pond, etc.). It will help you understand if a storm is headed your way.

PLAN FOR FIDO: Animals are often afterthoughts in a disaster. According to Jennifer Abbrecht of the Louisiana SPCA, "The worst thing you can do is leave your animal and hope for the best." During Hurricane Katrina, an estimated 80 percent of rescued animals were never reunited with their owners. Include your pets in your disaster plan from the outset and stock up on extra food and meds. Keep a carrying cage and pre-scout pet-friendly hotels or campgrounds in case you have to evacuate. Make sure your pets have tags or get them implanted with a scannable HomeAgain pet microchip.

HOW TO SHUT DOWN YOUR HOME IN FIVE MINUTES

NATURAL GAS

Most gas valves are located outside and require a wrench for shutoff. Consult your utility company for instructions on proper shutoff, then keep those instructions in an emergency drawer by the door with a wrench and a flashlight.

WATER

During a disaster, cracked exterior water lines can bring contaminated water into your house. To shut down your house's water, simply locate and turn off the main water valve, which typically is located in the basement.

ELECTRICITY

In a flood, live electrical outlets can become a danger to both your family and rescue workers. If flooding is possible, locate your main circuit box and shut off the main breaker. If there is already water in the basement, do not touch your service panel.

In October 2012, Hurricane Sandy caused massive flooding in the Northeast and claimed at least 40 lives.

Getting to Safety:

SHOULD YOU EVACUATE OR HUNKER DOWN? THE
ANSWER DEPENDS ON THE DISASTER YOU'RE FACING,
WHERE YOU LIVE, AND HOW MUCH TIME YOU HAVE.

YOUR CELLPHONE VIBRATES with an alert. A storm has been sighted. A bomb exploded. The fires can't be stopped. One of the most important parts of any survival situation is staying calm, knowing your options, and choosing the best of them in as little time as possible.

HURRICANE/FLOOD

"Getting people out of surge zones in time is critical," says Francisco Sanchez, an emergency-response manager in Houston. "So if there's an evacuation order, then go as fast as you safely can." Not in a surge zone? Consider riding it out at home, then evacuate afterward, if necessary.

HAZMAT/NUCLEAR EMERGENCY

Chemical plant fires, hazardous spills, and nuclear meltdowns are rare, Sanchez says, "but because of things like wind direction and weather patterns you need to follow very specific directions." Listen to the radio. If you are told to stay indoors, shut the windows, close the doors, kill the a/c, and get to an interior room. If instructions are to evacuate, keep the windows of your vehicle closed and the a/c off.

WILDFIRE

If a sheriff knocks on your door and tells you to leave, grab your family and go. Inspector Quvondo Johnson of the Los Angeles County Fire Department puts it like this: "Property is replaceable, lives aren't. We make predictions based on weather, dryness of brush, topography, and past fires. We try to give people as much time as possible, but when we say go, you should go."

TORNADO

A tornado watch from the National Weather Service means that there is a significant risk in your area. That gets upgraded to a tornado warning when the event is actually occurring and it means you'd better take cover in a hurry. If you don't have a basement or shelter, then get to a small room or closet in the interior of your house.

Expert Advice: Arthur Bradley, an engineer at NASA's Langley Research Center and author of the *Handbook to Practical Disaster Preparedness for the Family,* has found that a can of Crisco and a sheet of paper make an excellent long-term candle in a pinch. "Roll up the paper into a wick and stick the wick into the can," he says. It will burn for eight hours a day for a month.

19

HAZARD:
Structural Damage

Reentering your home—is it safe? Coming back to your house after an evacuation can be an emotional event—and a dangerous one, too. Seeing their homes and possessions damaged can cause people to act irrationally in what could be an unstable, toxic debris field. If your house has been knocked or floated off its foundation, don't go inside.

"If you hear shifting or unusual noises that signal that the structure may fall, leave immediately," says Francisco Sanchez of Houston's Harris County emergency management office. Same goes if you smell natural gas; get out quickly and call the gas company. Standing water from burst pipes or flooding can raise the risk of electrocution.

Have an electrician or the power company cut the power to your house before you mess with the water. If you see or smell mold, open your windows, then remove contaminated furniture or drywall. If you are on a municipal water supply, check with the town to see if the tap water's safe to drink. Stick to the bottled stuff until you're sure.

CHECKLIST: CLEANUP

You're going to have a lot of work to do after a disaster, so you'd better get geared up beforehand. Do you have:

☐ CHAINSAW

☐ GARBAGE BAGS

☐ DUST MASK

☐ EYE PROTECTION

☐ GLOVES

☐ BOOTS

☐ EARPLUGS

☐ CHAIN LUBE

☐ LOPPERS

☐ EXTRA CHAIN

☐ ROPE

☐ CROWBAR

→ **HAZARD:**
Guard Your Yard

Expensive things that live outside have a habit of disappearing in times of scarcity. Chain up and lock generators, grills, gas cans, and propane tanks to trees or to your deck to discourage looters. Nothing convenient to wrap a chain around? Feed a chain through a concrete block, then bury the block two feet deep to create a deadman anchor.

Expert Advice:

How to defend your home with a firearm. Towns hit by disaster can attract predators. If you own a gun and are trained to use it, this is a time to be vigilant but also restrained. **Mykel Hawke**, former Green Beret and host of *Elite Tactical Unit* on the Outdoor Channel, advocates giving any intruder three warnings:

1. State that you have a firearm.
2. Tell him you are licensed and trained with your weapon.
3. Say that you are afraid for your life and will shoot if he does not leave. "If an intruder persists, he is either insane or fully intent upon engaging you," says Hawke. "Either way, you have done your best to avoid conflict and must shoot until the threat is neutralized and you can call the authorities."

↯ HAZARD:

Can That Tree Hit My House?

Use a yardstick to find out. **1** Measure the distance between your eye and outstretched fist. **2** Grasp the yardstick at that distance and point it up. **3** Aim your fist at the base of the tree and move toward the house. If the top of the tree aligns with the top of the yardstick before you reach your house, your house is safe.

STRATEGY:

Tree Removal

CASE 1:
Leaning on a Structure

If that structure is your house, leave the tree alone—you want your insurance adjuster to see it. If it's on a shed or other outbuilding that doesn't meet a deductible, proceed carefully. According to Husqvarna Tree Expert Cary Shepherd, such trees can be under up-and-down as well as lateral pressure. That pressure could release in unexpected directions when you start to cut.

CASE 2:
Snagged on a Power Line

Don't touch any tree that's leaning on a power line and certainly don't have at it with a chainsaw. Trees are filled with water and are good conductors of electricity.

CASE 3:
On the Ground

Sounds like you've got some firewood coming your way. But work carefully. Watch for branches that are under tension. "Make sure you understand how that tree can twist or roll before cutting it," Shepherd says. "Ask yourself, what side will it roll on? You want to be on the opposite side."

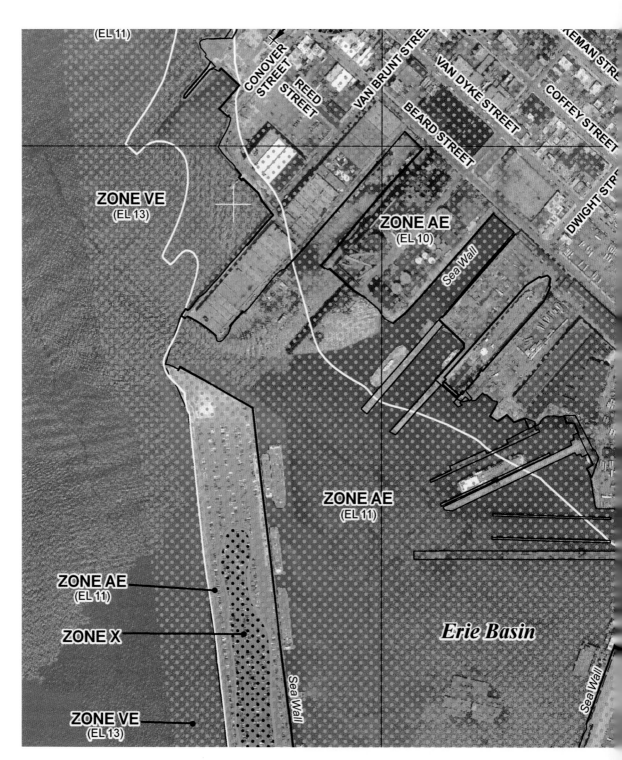

ZONE VE
(EL 13)

ZONE AE
(EL 10)

ZONE AE
(EL 11)

ZONE AE
(EL 11)

ZONE X

ZONE VE
(EL 13)

(EL 11)

CONOVER STREET

REED STREET

VAN BRUNT STREET

VAN DYKE STREET

BEARD STREET

COFFEY STREET

KEMAN STRE

DWIGHT STR

Sea Wall

Sea Wall

Sea Wall

Erie Basin

ZONE AE
(EL 10)

ZONE X

COLUMBIA

HENRY STREET

ON AVENUE

N AVENUE

LORRAINE STREET

BUSH STREET

CENTRE STREET

CREAMER STREET

HENRY STREET

BAY STREET

SIGOURNEY STREET

LLECK STREET

BAY STREET

CLINTON STREET

CREAMER STREET

ZONE AE
(EL 11)

ZONE X

Henry St Basin

Sea Wall

HALLECK
STREET

SMITH
STREET

COURT STREET

BRY

ZONE VE

← STRATEGY:
How to Read a FEMA Map:

Search for your address at msc.fema.gov. If your house is in a blue shaded area, you're in a 100-year-flood zone, which means there's a 1 percent chance of a flood of one foot or higher affecting your property in any given year.

The gray shaded zone puts you in the 500-year-flood risk category. Do you think FEMA got it wrong with your house? Check the base flood elevation on the map, then see if your house sits above that height.

RECOVERY

Two months. That's how long it took to get the power back on at the home of Jayne and Tom Lee in Breezy Point, New York, after Hurricane Sandy. The Lees are one of 37 families who were able to return to the neighborhood—more than 2,000 families remained displaced months later. For victims of a disaster, the return to normalcy can take a frustratingly long time after the rest of the world moves on. While you are still settling with the insurance company, protecting your property, and rebuilding your home, your responsibilities to your job, family, and friends don't go away. Welcome to the survival long game.

FOSTER GOODWILL: "The sense of community that comes out after a storm is incredible," says John Foberg, an HVAC engineer whose Hoboken, New Jersey, home was flooded after Sandy. Foberg's neighbors loaned him cleanup equipment and he gave back by turning his deck into a community barbecue spot.

SAY SO LONG TO YOUR CAR: If flooding reached over the floorboards of your vehicle, your insurer will consider it a total loss. The adjuster will quote you standard Blue Book value on the car, but double-check that number based on your area—and factor in any equipment you've installed.

DEALING WITH DEBRIS: All manner of wet, slippery, splintery junk will need to get shoveled, raked, and dragged to the curb. Wear protective gloves, boots, and long pants. Check with your town to see if there is a public debris removal program. If not, check with your insurer to see if your policy pays for a dumpster.

Dealing with Your Insurance Company

Take inventory.

You'll need to produce a detailed list of the stuff you had. Purva Patel, a journalist who reported on the insurance industry for the *Houston Chronicle* after Hurricanes Rita (2005) and Ike (2008), suggests using Cloud-based services such as the Insurance Information Institute's Home Inventory app and the National Association of Insurance Commissioners MyHOME Scr.APP.book.

Not so fast with the hammer.

"Do as little repair work as possible before the adjuster comes to your home," she advises. Document all the damage with photos and video. "You want to be able to show the agent how it started," she says.

Be tenacious.

Ask for copies of any documents and photos produced by the insurance company and adjuster. And keep calling until you get results. "A lot of adjusters are itinerant, not local," says Patel. "They move from storm to storm. So you've got to be persistent." If you feel you're being ignored, reach out to state regulators who monitor the industry.

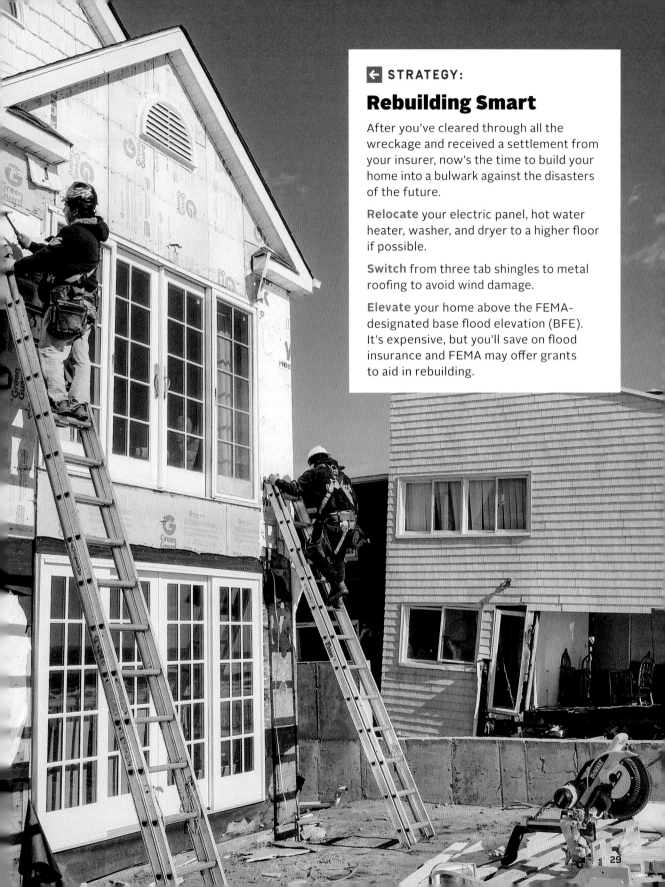

STRATEGY:

Rebuilding Smart

After you've cleared through all the wreckage and received a settlement from your insurer, now's the time to build your home into a bulwark against the disasters of the future.

Relocate your electric panel, hot water heater, washer, and dryer to a higher floor if possible.

Switch from three tab shingles to metal roofing to avoid wind damage.

Elevate your home above the FEMA-designated base flood elevation (BFE). It's expensive, but you'll save on flood insurance and FEMA may offer grants to aid in rebuilding.

Disaster-Proof Your Life

PROTECTING YOUR HOME AND FAMILY FROM CATASTROPHES IS A TASK BEST DONE BEFORE THE STORM CLOUDS GATHER. HERE'S HOW A TARGETED APPROACH TO DISASTER PREPARATION CAN REDUCE YOUR RISK.

FOR THE PAST few years, researchers at the Wharton Risk Management and Decision Processes Center at the University of Pennsylvania have been running a computer simulation to study how people choose to prepare for potential natural disasters. The simulation, called Quake, is a multiplayer game. All participants start out with a hypothetical $20,000 in cash and a house, and as the game progresses they must make decisions about how to use their money. A player can leave that money in the bank, earning a Madoff-like guaranteed annual return of 10 percent, or pay for structural improvements to help the house withstand an earthquake. The winner is the player with the highest net worth—cash plus the value of the house—at the end of the game, usually 10 virtual years.

Nearly everyone chooses to keep the money in the bank. The strange thing about this result is that the researchers, Howard Kunreuther and Robert Meyer, warn the players that quakes are highly likely—the game, after all, is called Quake. But players cling doggedly to that promised 10 percent rate of return. On occasion, the lab team has even told one of the players that the only way to win was to put the money into the house. Even then, he would typically delay for a couple of years, hoping to cash in before doing the home improvements. Then, predictably, an earthquake would come and wipe everyone out.

BEFORE TROUBLE STRIKES

The Quake study falls in the field of behavioral economics, in which over the past 30 years it has been determined that people often fail to make rational economic decisions. In general, it seems, people are too eager to lock in financial gains and too willing to gamble that losses will never materialize. If this is unfortunate when it comes to retirement savings, it is positively dangerous in a world riven by natural and man-made disasters. "People might be aware that there are going to be hurricanes or tornadoes or earthquakes," Meyer says, "but they think the actual

2009's Los Angeles Station Fire consumed 160,000 acres and destroyed 89 homes.

damage is something that happens to other people."

After Hurricane Katrina in 2005, a devastating Midwest tornado season in 2008, and deadly flooding in Tennessee, Mississippi, and Kentucky in May of 2010, public awareness of disasters is surely at a high point. A 2009 Red Cross study found that more than half of all Americans had personally experienced an emergency in which they'd either lost power for three days, had to evacuate, or had to provide serious first aid to others. Yet the same survey found that only 12 percent of Americans

had taken adequate disaster-preparedness steps.

However, as the 12 percent who do plan ahead can attest, most disaster prep is pretty straightforward stuff. Jeff Swiney, a towboat pilot from Lafayette, Louisiana, has seen three major hurricanes hit his home in the past 10 years. His strategy for weathering storms is easy to execute because everything has been fully planned out in advance. "Nothing's basic when a hurricane is blowing down your house," he says. "By then it's too late and that's when you see people fighting

An EF5 tornado devastated Greensburg, Kansas, in May 2007.

for the last bag of Doritos at the grocery store."

Once a person decides to take disaster preparation seriously, the first step is to assess the spectrum of threats. How would each type of disaster affect everything, from the structure of your home to the contents of your fridge?

From there, planning breaks down into two broad areas: general measures that apply to any situation and targeted tasks to protect against specific threats such as wildfires or hurricanes.

On the general side of the ledger, survival experts suggest that families plot escape routes and make sure that they know how to contact one another in a crisis. It makes sense to list all of the critical systems that support your daily life and home (hot water heater, boiler, water pump, phone, electricity, Internet) and learn how they work. Then you can create a backup plan in case they fail.

Once an immediate threat has passed, the survivors of any natural disaster need to focus on securing warmth, water, and food—and it doesn't have to be difficult.

THE NEXT DAY

Heat and electricity sound like two different challenges, but both needs can be satisfied by a generator and fuel. During almost any natural disaster, the power may go out and stay out for a while. In such a situation, generators can seem like miracles. In warm climates, a backup generator keeps food cool and your lights and a/c running. In cold weather, generators can power either electric space heaters or fuel pumps to keep oil burners running. But you can't just buy any generator, stick it in the garage, and expect to reap the benefits when the lights go dark.

Selecting and using this machine is an exercise in load management. Before you shop, figure out which household appliances you want to keep running, the electrical load (in watts) that each one draws, and how many hours per day they need to operate. Many retailers feature generator calculators to help you pick the right model.

Once you get the generator home, be sure to operate it safely. To avoid carbon-monoxide poisoning, never run a generator in an enclosed space—set it up outside and away from open windows and a/c vents. Large generators work best when wired directly into your home's circuitry. Consider hiring an electrician to install a transfer switch so you don't have to plug individual appliances in separately.

After shelter, water is the most pressing need in times of disaster. Most of us can't survive more than three days without it and natural disasters often knock water-treatment plants offline. During floods, contaminated water can also back-flow into household water pipes. That means that an army of microbes is just waiting to infect your gut at exactly the time when local hospitals are likely to be overwhelmed. Treating water is easy: Strain it, then boil for one minute or treat with chlorine bleach (one tablespoon for 10 gallons) and you'll kill off most pathogens. But it's better to think ahead by keeping a three-day supply of bottled water (one gallon per person per day) on hand. Cody Lundin, survival instructor and author of *When All Hell Breaks Loose,* takes it a step further. If disaster looms, he suggests filling everything in the house—from bathtubs to one-gallon ziplock bags—with tap water before contamination begins.

Food is the least essential of the survival essentials. People have been known to survive three long weeks without food. But who wants to go through that kind of suffering? As with water, it's relatively easy to build up a supply of food just by buying some extra dried beans, Campbell's soup, and dried fettuccine every time you shop. Soon you'll be stocked up with little pain to the billfold.

If you've lost power, open your fridge only when you absolutely need to and your food will stay pretty cold—especially if you can power it for a couple of hours every day with a generator. If you have time before the bad weather hits, organize your fridge, putting the most perishable food toward the front, and save the stuff in the freezer for last.

Securing your heat, water, and food may be the starting point of disaster prep—but turning your home into a real bulwark against disaster takes more effort. Study FEMA maps to determine the disaster profile of your area and learn as much as you can about how floods, hurricanes, wildfires, and other dangerous events can affect your house and neighborhood. Then invest your time, energy, and money accordingly. You might build structural reinforcements in case of an earthquake or practice smart landscaping to defend against a wildfire—such measures are detailed elsewhere on these pages. And remember the lesson of Quake and similar studies: When it comes to natural disasters, the biggest risk is assuming that they can never happen to you.

In an emergency, a generator is one of your most important pieces of equipment.

THE THREAT: Millions of acres of the U.S. burn each year.
WHERE: Sunbelt states and Alaska
WHEN: June to September

WILDFIRE

Don't confuse a house fire with a wildland fire that's about to overrun your house. If you didn't evacuate earlier—and you probably should have—your house is where you make your final stand. Shutting your windows against flying embers is an obvious step, but just as important is to open the fireplace damper to ventilate deadly gas and smoke that will precede the fire. Make sure to shut off gas or propane lines, but stop there. "Don't shut off the water—we can use that—and don't shut off the electricity," says Fred Stowers, a 30-year veteran of the Los Angeles County Fire Department, who helped combat 2009's 160,000-acre Station Fire. "Turn lights on so we can see inside and tell the difference between things like drifting smoke and roaring flames."

Keep Your Home Safe from Fire

1. Make sure tree crowns are at least 10 feet apart.

2. Clear all flammable vegetation within a 15-foot perimeter.

3. Thin out trees and shrubs to the property edge.

THE THREAT:
400,000 fires each year
kill almost 3,000 and
injure more than 14,000.
WHERE: Anywhere
WHEN: Most common
in winter months

HOUSE FIRE

More Americans die in house fires every year than in all natural disasters combined. When in doubt, escape the building, but if you judge that you can safely mount a fire-extinguisher battle, there are two rules you need to know. Rule one: Stay six feet from the flames so you don't torch the rest of your house by air-blasting a nascent fire across the room. Rule two: People often forget rule one and make things worse, so keep your escape route to your back when you pull the trigger. More than 50 percent of fatal house fires occur between 11:00 p.m. and 7:00 a.m. (peak hours for all fires are 5:00 p.m. to 8:00 p.m.), so practice two ways out of every room at night. And make sure at least one of them does not rely on a stairwell, which can easily become a deadly vortex of gas, smoke, heat, and flame. "Homes are the only occupancy in the country allowed by code to have an open staircase," says house-fire expert John Norman, a retired chief for the Fire Department of New York. "We call them chimneys. They serve as channels for fire as it moves upward." Finally, it may sound basic, but picking an outside rendezvous point is critical so you can discover quickly who's made it out of the house and who hasn't.

The 2003 Northeast blackout shut down 10 major cities, including New York (pictured), where thousands of subway passengers had to be evacuated.

BLACKOUT

THE THREAT: Recent large-scale power outages have lasted up to three weeks.
WHERE: Anywhere
WHEN: Outages spike in summer, when a/c demand is high.

Power outages are a routine side effect of other disasters, but sometimes a blackout can be a disaster in itself. The largest recent example in the United States was, of course, the Northeast blackout of 2003, which left 50 million people without power and caused 11 deaths. All told, it caused six billion dollars in damage. That blackout was widespread, but it was hardly an isolated incident. On average, a dozen large-scale blackouts affecting at least 50,000 people each occur every year. Like many disasters, blackouts introduce issues of food spoilage, water contamination, and exposure to heat and cold that only get more severe as the outage lingers. The best defense is a generator, but it's also important to keep a flashlight and radio where you can easily find them. In widespread blackouts, communication networks tend to suffer along with the grid. Landline and cell networks can get overwhelmed, but short texts will get through. A useful and free service called I'm Ok lets you create an emergency contact list so you can send mass emails with a single text message.

BLIZZARD

THE THREAT: Winter storms can paralyze whole regions.
WHERE: Everywhere but the Southern U.S.
WHEN: December to April

Severe winter storms can snow people in for days at a time while heavy ice and snow routinely bring down tree limbs and power lines. Homeowners in cold-weather states are used to breaking out the shovels (and even the roof rakes) for the hard task of snow removal. But a clear driveway isn't an excuse for a drive—70 percent of winter storm fatalities occur in automobiles—so sit tight at home and stay warm. If the power's out, a generator will help keep the basic utilities running. But if you lack backup power and think you may be in it for the long haul, set up a "camp" inside your house with a tent, sleeping bags, and your family all shut in in a single room to consolidate heat. Long-lasting cold can burst water pipes, so prepare the house by turning off the water supply at the source, then open the lowest faucet and drain your pipes. But be sure to save some water for drinking, cooking, and cleaning—eating snow is a dangerous way to hydrate and can lead to a case of hypothermia.

TIP! DON'T FORGET YOUR TOILET

Pour RV-grade antifreeze or, in a pinch, vodka into the toilet trap to prevent freezing.

Tornadoes can produce winds of 250 mph or higher. In April 2010, a deadly Mississippi tornado traveled more than 140 miles.

Anatomy of a Safe Room

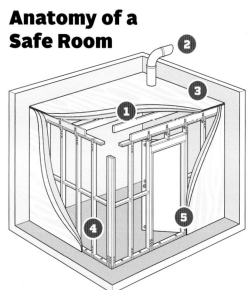

1. Walls are constructed of two layers of plywood and one layer of 14-gauge steel.

2. Ventilation ducts allow pressure to equalize.

3. Structure takes advantage of foundation walls but does not attach to house.

4. Studs are strapped to plates.

5. Steel doors close securely with triple deadbolts.

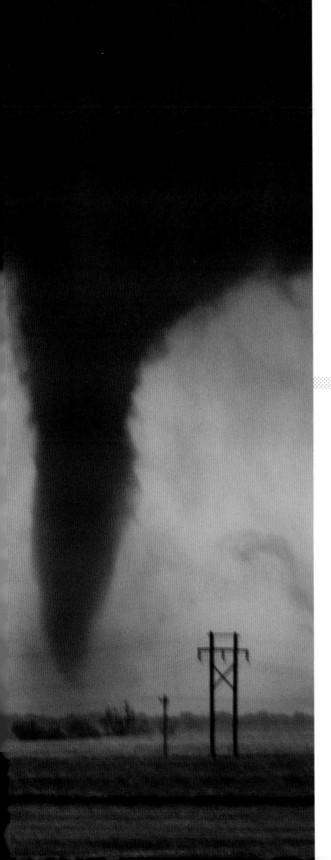

TORNADO

THE THREAT:
Approximately 1,000
tornadoes hit the U.S.
each year.
WHERE: Most common
in Plains states
WHEN: Spring and
summer, usually in early
evening

Tornado fundamentals are easy: Get to the lowest floor in the house and put as many walls as possible between you and the twister. In tornado country, residents often install underground or basement storm shelters. For homeowners who lack basements, researchers at Texas Tech University have developed plans for DIY aboveground safe rooms created by pouring concrete into foam forms. Plans for DIY retrofit shelters, such as the basement build-in pictured here, can be found at fema.gov. If a tornado catches you out in the open, conventional wisdom is to hide in a ditch, but Larry J. Tanner, one of the researchers at Texas Tech who has investigated every major U.S. tornado in the past 12 years, disagrees. "You'll never see me in one," he says. "I've seen all sorts of things in ditches after a tornado—2 x 4s, propane tanks, rolled cars." Look for a covered culvert instead. "If you're in a city, stay away from grocery stores, gymnasiums, or anything with a long roof span. Take shelter in large, sturdy buildings: Banks and hospitals are usually good."

FLOODING

THE THREAT: Floods cause an average five billion dollars in losses and 100 fatalities yearly—about 3,800 towns are on floodplains.
WHERE: Mainly coastal states and the Mississippi River Valley
WHEN: Spring and fall

Sump pumps are the best defense against minor flooding and chronically wet basements, but if a river is rising nearby or a coastal storm surge is imminent, the best advice is to move your valuables to a high floor, then evacuate. And if there are flash-flood warnings, be quick about it. These floods move fast and tend to carry mud, trees, and other dangerous debris with them. If you're in a flood zone—check your address with the FEMA Map Service Center (msc.fema.gov) to find out— plan an escape route ahead of time. And never drive through moving water; it can be a death trap. Almost 50 percent of flood fatalities are car-related. Don't be lulled into a false sense of security by the term "100-year flood" either. That doesn't indicate that a flood will occur only once a century. What it really means is that every single year there's a one-in-100 chance of that level of flooding. If you live in a flood zone, the U.S. Geological Survey estimates that you've got a one-in-two chance of experiencing a flood in your lifetime.

An SUV sits submerged in floodwater covering downtown streets and sidewalks on May 3, 2010, in Nashville Tennessee. More than 13 inches of rain fell over two days, leaving at least seven dead and thousands displaced.

Check Your Sump Pump

1. Every few months remove the cover to your sump pump well and slowly pour water into the tank.

2. If water pours back into the tank, you may need to replace the check valve.

3. Watch to ensure that the float rises with the water and triggers the pump.

Quake-Proof Your Water Heater

1. Create two belts around the tank with ¾-inch plumber's tape.

2. Crimp a ½-inch-diameter electrical metallic tubing (EMT) conduit at both ends, then attach to plumber's-tape belt and studs with screws.

3. Attach water and gas lines with flexible connectors.

A portion of highway 5 in California collapsed after a magnitude 6.7 earthquake hit outside of Los Angeles in 1994.

EARTHQUAKE

THE THREAT: The most destructive recent U.S. quake (Northridge, California, 1994) caused $40 billion in damage and killed 61. **WHERE:** California and the Midwest **WHEN:** At least one great quake (magnitude 8.0 and up) hits somewhere in the world each year.

Today there is no credible way to predict earthquakes, so when a big one hits a U.S. population center—and experts agree that there will be a big one—it will come without warning and it will be devastating. Most modern houses are bolted to their foundations, but older houses may be held in place simply by their own weight. To earthquake-proof an older home, spend a few hundred dollars on half-inch anchor bolts and earthquake brackets to attach your home to its foundation and keep it from shaking or sliding free. Also remember to secure major appliances and freestanding bookshelves to the walls and install flexible gas and water lines to prevent ruptures or leaks. Those busted lines can make the fiery aftermath of an earthquake just as deadly as the quake itself. If you smell gas, get out of your house immediately and keep an eye out for downed power lines. Finally, the most useful technology to have around after an earthquake could be an old-fashioned battery-powered radio. "The power grid will be down and the cell grid will be overwhelmed," says Mary Lou Zoback, a geophysicist with Risk Management Solutions. "It's going to be your lifeline for information."

HURRICANE

THE THREAT: Each year there are six to eight hurricanes, causing an average five billion dollars in damage per season.
WHERE: Eastern and Southern coastal states
WHEN: Summer and fall; September is the cruelest month

The most important thing to have in place for hurricane season is a plan to get out of town. Tow-boat captain and 28-year Coast Guard veteran Jeff Swiney has had multiple hurricanes hit his Lafayette, Louisiana, home and he knows a thing or two about disaster evacuation. "You've got to have predetermined trigger points and then act on them," he says. "Too many people wait until it's too late, when the storm is overwhelming, and that's when they get hurt." Second only to the safety of your family should be the structural integrity of your home. The best time to build in hurricane protection is during new construction, when roof straps and permanent storm shutters can be added with little additional effort. But existing roofs can be retrofitted with gable end braces and temporary storm shutters can be cut to fit in a couple of hours. Don't forget to bolster your garage as well, Swiney says—he braces the entrance with diagonally placed 2 x 4s. "Garage doors are weak," he says. "And if a hurricane-force wind gets inside, it will take your whole roof off."

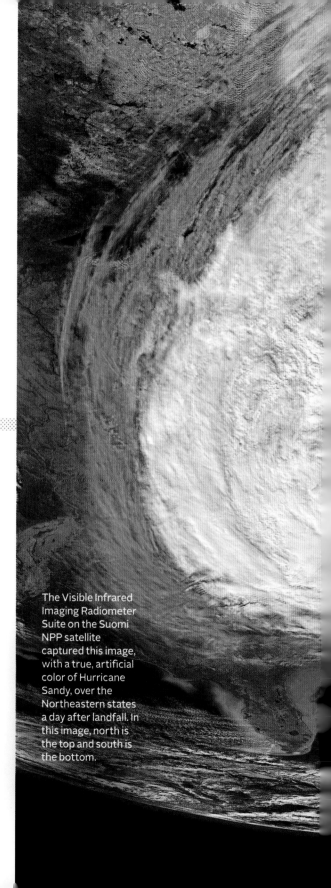

The Visible Infrared Imaging Radiometer Suite on the Suomi NPP satellite captured this image, with a true, artificial color of Hurricane Sandy, over the Northeastern states a day after landfall. In this image, north is the top and south is the bottom.

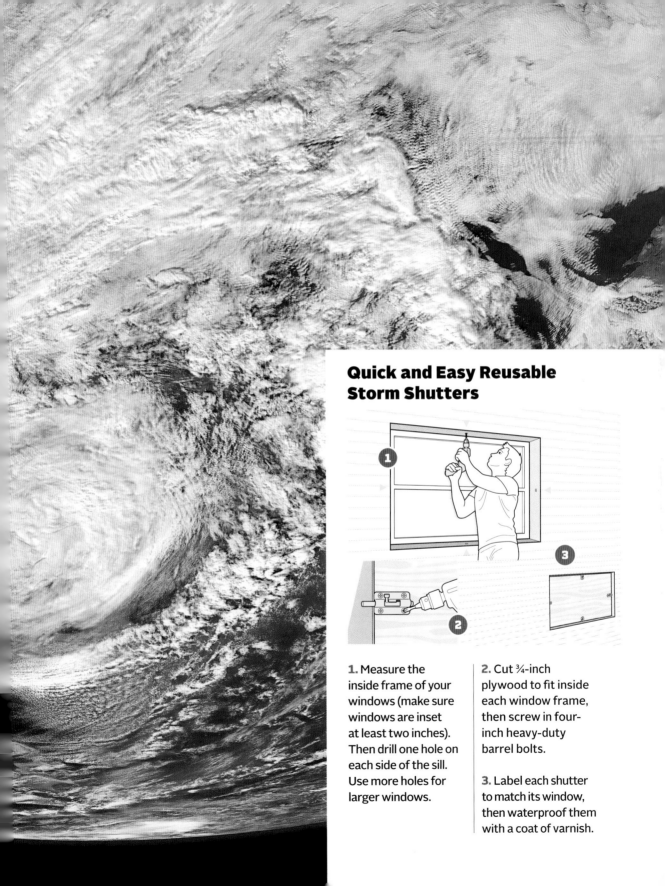

Quick and Easy Reusable Storm Shutters

1. Measure the inside frame of your windows (make sure windows are inset at least two inches). Then drill one hole on each side of the sill. Use more holes for larger windows.

2. Cut ¾-inch plywood to fit inside each window frame, then screw in four-inch heavy-duty barrel bolts.

3. Label each shutter to match its window, then waterproof them with a coat of varnish.

Prepping Lite

WHAT PREPPERS DO, AND WHAT YOU, A SLIGHTLY
LESS PARANOID CITIZEN, CAN DO.

COMMUNICATION

Prepper: Establish a *dead drop*—a secret place to deposit and retrieve messages when communications go down. Tell only trusted confidants about this place.

Casual survivalist: Get your ham-radio license. Plenty of people still use ham radios to communicate, including FEMA. In a catastrophe, it might be your only option.

HEAT

Prepper: If the power goes out, a woodstove is great backup. Better solution: an outdoor wood furnace that connects to your home's existing heating system.

Casual survivalist: Store a couple of ceramic flowerpots in the closet. Two pots nested, turned upside down, and propped above a few candles make an effective space heater.

SHELTER

Prepper: Build an underground bunker. Ideally, for ultimate secrecy, not on your house property. But that might also require a rather large purchase.

Casual survivalist: Have a list of emergency shelters. They should be accessible and sturdy—a public shelter, a church, or your neighbor's basement, which also has a pool table.

FOOD

Prepper: Practice hunting the animals native to your area. Worth noting: Domesticated rabbits are less gamy than their wild counterparts.

Casual survivalist: Nonfood items you should have in your emergency pantry: manual can opener, Flintstones multivitamins, and Sterno (for cooking).

HEALTH

Prepper: A properly equipped go bag, or bug-out bag, is heavy. Establish a training regimen on various terrains so that you can flee without getting winded.

Casual survivalist: Pick up a fitness tracker. In a low-food situation, it'll track your vitals and even count your calories. In the meantime, you'll just be healthier.

WATER

Prepper: Capacity of your cistern equals (one gallon per person) x (number of people) x (number of days of expected cataclysm) x (10—just to be safe).

Casual survivalist: Keep a large water-filter pitcher in your fridge. Good for everyday use and as a filtration system. At the first sign of trouble, fill all extra containers and the bathtub.

CHECKLIST:

Ideal Survival Kits

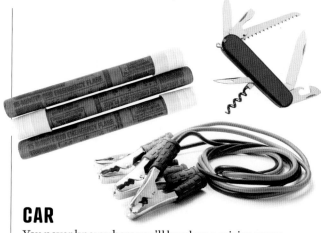

A **WELL-STOCKED DISASTER** kit can save lives in a crisis. Relief agencies recommend that homeowners keep three days' worth of food and water as well as a kit of medical supplies and other essentials in the house at all times. However, *Popular Mechanics* recommends that our readers go a step further. Outlined at right are three disaster kits—one for your home, one for your car, and one in a backpack for quick evacuations. That way, when disaster strikes and there's no time to think, you won't have to.

CAR

You never know where you'll be when a crisis occurs, so keep a box of supplies in the trunk of your car to sustain your family if stranded on the road.

- ☐ Local maps and road atlas
- ☐ Writing supplies (pencils, pens, notebook)
- ☐ Food (e.g., dried fruit, snacks, cookies)
- ☐ Two gallons bottled water
- ☐ Mess kit (paper cups, plates, utensils)
- ☐ Compact sleeping bag or blankets
- ☐ Sanitation supplies (toilet paper, moist towelettes, garbage bags, plastic ties)
- ☐ Hand sanitizer
- ☐ Duct tape
- ☐ Cellphone car charger
- ☐ Clothes (sweater, waterproof jacket, hat, shoes)
- ☐ First-aid kit (bandages, antibiotic ointment, antiseptic, aspirin, antidiarrheal medicine, medical tape)
- ☐ Multitool or knife
- ☐ Fire extinguisher
- ☐ Jumper cables
- ☐ Light sticks or roadside flares
- ☐ Towline for hauling or towing

BACKPACK

In an emergency evacuation, there's not always time to find what you need, so your grab-and-go pack should be preloaded with all your essentials.

☐ Important documents (copy of insurance policies, identification, bank records, medical records, copies of deeds)

☐ Prescriptions (medication, eyeglasses)

☐ Mini first-aid kit (bandages, antibiotic ointment, aspirin)

☐ $300 cash (in small denominations)

☐ Prepaid phone card

☐ Matches in waterproof container

☐ Flashlight and extra batteries

☐ Whistle to signal for help

☐ Portable NOAA weather radio (battery or hand-crank powered)

☐ Food (e.g., granola, nuts) and bottled water

☐ Extra set of keys for your home and car

☐ Infant/child necessities

HOME

The supplies in your home should keep your family safe and healthy for at least three days—and be useful during the cleanup phase.

☐ Window-sealing materials (plastic sheeting, duct tape)

☐ Change of clothing

☐ Food, including for your pets

☐ One gallon of water per person per day and bleach (to sanitize water)

☐ Can opener, plastic utensils, plates

☐ Lantern or candles and matches

☐ Flashlight with extra batteries

☐ NOAA weather radio

☐ Dust masks

☐ Fire extinguisher

☐ Heavy gloves for removing debris

☐ Rope

☐ First-aid kit and manual

☐ Disinfectant and hand sanitizer

☐ Toilet paper and bucket

☐ Hand and power tools (generator, fuel, chainsaw, shovel, rake, buckets, hose, hatchet, knife, hammer, broom, drill/driver, circular saw, fully charged backup batteries for tools)

TALES OF SURVIVAL:

"Nothing is Impossible for Those Who Fight"

A COUNTRY'S TALE OF SURVIVAL. *POPULAR MECHANICS* GOES TO CUBA AND FINDS A PEOPLE DEVOTED TO HARD WORK AND INGENUITY—OFTEN BY NECESSITY.

BY KEVIN DUPZYK

ON OUR SECOND day in Cuba, we saw in one humdrum, 10-minute transaction a clue to the way life is lived in a country where daily life is often a challenge.

We had hired a man called Francel to drive us from Trinidad, a 500-year-old town on Cuba's south shore, to Varadero, a resort town three and a half hours northwest. Francel was tall and thin and wore black, just like his car, a mid-1990s Peugeot. At 20 years old, it looked boxy and dated, but it was newer and in better shape than most cars in the country—it's not like everyone in Cuba drives a well-preserved American classic the way you hear about. The Peugeot's floor mats were red plastic with a diamond-plate pattern. The air conditioning worked and so did the seat belts, both noteworthy. Every window was tinted dark with the exception of small cutouts so Francel could see the side-view mirrors. Inexplicably, the cutouts were the shape of the Apple logo.

Just outside Trinidad, Francel pulled off the road into the side yard of a small house. A man with no shirt on sat on a chair out front, just sitting. Francel drove around back into a small parking space under a split-rail carport with corrugated-steel siding. At the next house over, across a small field, I saw a pig and a chicken lazing in the sun. The man from the front appeared and retrieved a gas can.

They barely spoke to each other, Francel and this man. They were operating within an invisible system. This transaction was, in fact, part of the vast and intricate web of improvised systems that constitutes the only way Cuba truly functions. Multiple generations of life with rationed food, little money, and a government set on isolation have produced a resourceful people. We humans are indeed a creative little animal and we find ways to help ourselves. Where I live, we have the luxury of exercising creativity for fun. In Cuba, they have to be creative just to live.

Once the man had finished filling the tank of the Peugeot, Francel fired up the car and we drove off. I noticed the fuel gauge on his car didn't work. "How do you know when you're empty?" I asked.

He laughed.

MY FRIENDS AND I traveled to Cuba on a sort of curiosity vacation. We wanted to see Cuba before the country's newly normalized relations with the United States became truly normal. In America the maker movement is at its height, a wave of people building and making and creating things with technologies that improve by the day. In Cuba, they've had a maker movement since 1960, fueled largely by necessity. I wanted to see if the instincts were the same.

We spent our first three days in Havana in a *casa particular,* a private home that rents rooms to tourists. It works much like Airbnb, but it's a system the Cuban government formalized in 1997. We had booked a room in Casa Leticia, one of the most highly rated casas in Vedado, which, according to the Internet, is the hippest neighborhood in Havana.

A cab from the airport dropped us off in front of the casa. The houses here were built right up to the crumbling sidewalks, two or three stories high, and wore faded paint stripped to dirty pastel shades by the salty ocean air. An old man in a red Havana Club vest sat alone on the sidewalk. Two skinny dogs lay on their sides panting. I thought there'd been a mistake. We double-checked the address. We were in the right place. Upon closer examination I saw a sticker above the door of the inauspicious building that was Casa Leticia: "2014 Winner, TripAdvisor Certificate of Excellence."

We rang the doorbell and Leticia herself opened the gate. A large, sunny interior courtyard was paved with perfect ceramic tile, lush with greenery, and outfitted with white wrought-iron patio furniture. A peristyle surrounded the courtyard, yellow-painted columns complementing green-and-blue-striped awnings hung between them. Inside, the immaculate house had ornately painted twenty-foot ceilings and—crucially, it would turn out—a bathroom, complete with shiny new fixtures.

Leticia, who was in her fifties, was short with blond hair and fair skin. Her eyes never stopped smiling and dimples appeared on her cheeks when she talked. She funneled us toward the dining room, where we filled out the simple paperwork that logged our stay. Then she opened a handsomely decorated liquor cabinet in the corner of the room and produced three glasses and a bottle of Havana Club, poured us each a shot, and gave us advice for our stay or for life or both.

"You are three young men. Watch out for *chicas.* There is no such thing as love at first sight.

"You will come across people who are very impressive. Well traveled. They will speak multiple languages and know places to take you. But when you get to the end of the day and you've paid for everything, they're gone.

"You are here because of the new Obama laws. Visit Cuba with an open mind."

Leticia had a system for everything.

HAVANA IS A great crumbling beauty in a constant state of repair. Walking through the neighborhood near Leticia's house, we saw some men pulling cinder blocks uphill on a wooden pallet outfitted with casters and a handle made of bent rebar. First appearances—appearances in general—are deceiving. We came to learn that the old man with the red vest was a government employee, hired to watch cars overnight. Men in red vests were stationed around the city, standing guard over the population of famed American classics and less familiar foreign makes like Lada, made in Russia, and Geely, which is Chinese. Buildings in the city seemed to grow taller as they approached the water, where a great walkable boulevard called the Malecón traces the shore. Like Casa Leticia, many buildings were pitiable on the outside but astonishing on the inside. According to our guidebook, three buildings collapse per day. When their guts spill out, I'm sure they are beautiful.

Our first night we had dinner with a computer programmer named Medardo Rodriguez. I had read about an entrepreneurship club he ran and contacted him before our trip. Medardo met us at the Hotel Nacional, one of the few buildings whose outside is as immaculate as the inside. It sits on a bluff over Havana Bay, outdoor seating arranged around two incongruous bits of decor: cannons from the armory that preceded the hotel on the site and an art installation riffing on bathrooms. A porcelain toilet stood on a tiled and graffitied pedestal. A lifeguard tower had a commode for a chair. Creative reclamation.

Medardo was older than I'd expected for the leader of a group devoted to developing a startup culture where virtually none exists. Balding and pushing 40, he wore trendy plastic glasses and bounced while he walked. He reminded me of a grizzled Silicon Valley veteran who'd survived the dot-com bubble with his enthusiasm for technology intact.

At the restaurant Medardo explained his role in the Merchise Startup Circle, the organization trying to engage and develop entrepreneurs in Cuba. The group grew out of a programming collective Medardo founded at the University "Marta Abreu" of Las Villas in central Cuba in the early 1990s. He taught programming as a practice of creative thinking. The group developed video games and even a web browser, but broke up in the early 2000s. It is difficult to maintain a programming collective in a country where the number of citizens with access to the Internet hovers at around 5 percent.

That hasn't stopped the group from reforming under a new guise. Creative thinking properly focused is entrepreneurship. And to Medardo, being disconnected from the rest of the world has in fact been the very stimulus of his most creative thinking. He learned from programming that being connected can be a distraction. Perhaps, he wondered, programmers learn better without the buzzing Internet constantly robbing their attentiveness. How easily might someone else's creativity replace our own if we let it?

As we were eating and talking, life in the courtyard suddenly stopped. The space had been full of the din of other tables and friends, a vending-

In Cuba, when a system doesn't exist, they make one.

machine hum, the clatter of the kitchen. Suddenly, silence. The power had gone out.

"Now you are knowing the real Cuba," Medardo said.

As workers retrieved portable lights, we strangers simultaneously pulled out our smartphones, turned on their flashlights, and placed them on the table. Someone said the light was too harsh. "Use the saltshaker," said a voice in the crowd. My friend put one over his phone's light. The crystals softened its glow. Each of us who could find a saltshaker did the same, and, just like that, we invented mood lighting.

AFTER HAVANA WE visited Trinidad, a colonial town with cobblestone streets. We stayed at Casa Balbina, where our host, Ricardo, was a retired chemistry professor. I told him I worked for an American magazine called *Popular Mechanics*, and he laughed and explained that Cuba used to have a magazine called *Mecánica Popular*. Ricardo had to be in his eighties, old enough to have read *Mecánica Popular,* the Spanish-language edition of *Popular Mechanics*, before the embargo started in 1960. I've heard some older Cubans still have collections of them. They might be on the shelf next to *Con Nuestros Propios Esfuerzos* ("With Our Own Efforts"), a government publication from the post–Soviet era that provided shop notes for Cubans trying to get by as their economy collapsed. In *Popular Mechanics*, the motto for our Shop Notes section is "Easy Ways to Do Hard Things." *Con Nuestros Propios Esfuerzos* also has a motto, from Fidel Castro: "Nothing Is Impossible for Those Who Fight."

In early 1960 *Mecánica Popular* split into two local editions: one for South America and one for Mexico and the Caribbean. Trinidad feels like a city paused in that moment. Built on an easy slope up from the Caribbean shore, it is an anthill of workers. A man cut tile on a table saw in the dark anteroom of his home. Another tossed cinder blocks from a cart on the street to a fellow working inside. The cobblestones had been removed from a hillside street to make way for plumbing work. On another street neat stacks of stones cordoned off a repaving project, the way bright orange cones would be used in the United States. In Cuba, when a system doesn't exist, they make one.

Trudging uphill to make a dinner reservation, we saw a man working alone on a red brick wall. He spread mortar in thick gray slabs and placed bricks in an alternating pattern—header, stretcher, header, stretcher. It was hot and sweaty work on a hot and sweaty day, but he wore protective long sleeves and pants and a work belt. He reminded me of the construction workers on the tract homes in Sacramento, California, where I grew up. The summer sun routinely pushed temperatures above 100 degrees, but practicality outweighed comfort. They wore jeans and long flannel.

We ate dinner at a *paladar*, a privately owned restaurant that was part of a formalized system analogous to that of the casas particulares. The waiters were trained by the state-owned catering company. They were dressed formally and brought out entrées on platters covered with silver lids, which they removed from everyone's dish at exactly the same time.

Over dinner we talked about what we had seen and what we had not seen. We had been to multiple restaurants that ordered only a small portion of the items on their menus. We had tried to visit museums and been foiled by idiosyncratic schedules. We had made an attempt to buy a wireless Internet card at the state telecom office during a service outage. "The most productive person we've seen was throwing bricks," one of my friends said.

Part of the fascination of seeing men perform manual labor in Cuba is that, unlike in the U.S., the other options are less obvious and the work itself seemed to animate the people doing it. We had seen plenty of Cubans who had jobs in air-conditioned rooms: rental-car clerks, people who worked in stores. In the U.S. those would be seen as better jobs than building a brick wall. On this street in Trinidad, the opposite felt true.

After dinner—chicken and lamb with a buffet of sides like rice and beans and tropical fruits—when we were walking home, we saw the bricklayer's wall nearly finished.

IT'S FUNNY, I almost didn't get to go to Cuba at all. My two buddies went through Cuban immigration without a hitch. I didn't have any problems at first, but when my suitcase went through the scanner, it raised a red flag. I had brought 17 copies of the June issue of *Popular Mechanics*, thinking I would meet people who might like it—people who've managed to maintain a 1950 Chevrolet for sixty-five years, or who keep buildings from turning to rubble, or who've cast livelihoods from the raw materials of everyday life. People who have learned to improvise to the point where improvisation becomes the way to keep living. But I'd overlooked the possibility that a suitcase full of American magazines might look like propaganda, especially considering that the headline on the cover of the "Maker Nation" issue I'd brought was "How *You* Can Join the Revolution."

The first customs agent asked if I spoke Spanish (no). She brought over a second agent with better English to ask me to explain myself. I tried to articulate what *Popular Mechanics* is about, then I tried to make up a story about giving the magazines to my friends to take home, but the language barrier made it difficult— and, also, that made no sense. Seeing the commotion, a third agent came over and immediately started examining the magazine. Things began to turn. I continued arguing my case, but now I was watching this third agent. He flipped through the magazine, stopping on all the best pages: the beautiful things, the projects, the makers. I struggled for words. He saw something he recognized.

Make a Fire Starter

Save up your dryer lint over the course of a few loads. Take an empty paper egg carton and pack each pod with a plug of the lint. Melt cheap or half-spent candles in a pot. Pour melted wax over each pod. Allow it to dry, then cut each pod out of the carton. Throw a couple of pods beneath some kindling in your campfire and they'll start a fire nicely.

2.

Threat: Low

THERE'S NOTHING TO WORRY ABOUT. YOU'RE
JUST BEING CAUTIOUS. LEARNING AND PREPARING.

The Four Safest Cities

TAKING INTO ACCOUNT NUCLEAR FALLOUT, NATURAL DISASTERS, EXTREME WEATHER, PROXIMITY TO FRESH WATER, AND EVEN VIOLENT-CRIME STATISTICS. ANOTHER BENEFIT: THEY'RE ALL QUITE LOVELY.

1.
SITKA, ALASKA

The big advantage: You're already used to being isolated. Surprisingly mild year-round, despite being in Alaska. An abundance of wild food sources.

2.
MISSOULA, MONTANA

Surrounding mountains keep extreme weather at bay. Very low threat of natural disasters. The Clark Fork River runs right through town.

3.
HURRICANE, UTAH

Unfortunate name, yes. But its desert climate will suit cold weather haters. Two nearby reservoirs and the Virgin River provide water.

4.
WHEELING, WEST VIRGINIA

No major hurricane, earthquake, or tornado threats. Far enough south to avoid lake effect snowfall. The moonshine keeps you warm.

Missoula,
Montana

Four Summertime Hazards

NEW WAYS TO SURVIVE THE WILDEST OUTDOOR SEASON UNSCATHED.

MOSQUITOS!

DEET is still the gold-standard chemical for hiding from mosquitoes, but the latest products also trick the bloodsuckers' sensory abilities. Carbon dioxide–emitting traps such as the Mosquito Magnet Patriot Mosquito Trap lure mosquitoes to their doom. There's also the new Mosquito Bait & Kill from Terminix AllClear, which coats plants and backyard surfaces in garlic oil and sugar for up to four weeks. (The sugar attracts them, the garlic oil kills them.)

POISON IVY!

Even if you tear it out by hand, poison ivy is likely to return. To kill a vine for good, spray it during its peak growth cycle, late spring and summer, with Roundup Poison Ivy Plus Tough Brush, which contains both glyphosate and a surfactant, which helps the glyphosate penetrate the surface of the leaves. If you can't find that, try Ortho Max Poison Ivy & Tough Brush Killer Concentrate. A greener option: Rent a goat. They eat the stuff.

WET CELLPHONES!

If your pool party is any kind of fun, someone is going to end up in the water with his cellphone in his pocket. To save it, turn it off and wipe it down immediately. Try placing the phone in a desiccant bag, such as the Bheestie Bag, which will remove moisture using the same technology as the Do Not Eat packets that come with shoes. Do not turn your phone back on for at least 24 hours. It'll short.

DRY BURGERS!

To keep precious fat from leaching out of your burgers and onto the coals, Josh Capon, chef of Burger & Barrel in Manhattan and six-time winner of the Burger Bash at the New York City Wine & Food Festival, recommends loose patties, a half-inch or more in thickness, using meat with a 75:25 lean:fat ratio. Cook for about four minutes on each side over direct heat. And stop playing with them.

Burdock flowers are pretty. Their roots are delicious.

STRATEGY:
HOW TO IDENTIFY PLANTS

WHEN YOU'RE HUNGRY, THE WOODS OFFER THEIR OWN VARIETY OF FRESH PRODUCE. YOU JUST NEED TO KNOW WHAT TO PICK.

THREE YOU CAN EAT

WILD WATERCRESS
WHEN: Early spring and fall
HOW TO CONSUME: Put it in a salad, like lettuce

CHICKWEED
WHEN: Early spring
HOW TO CONSUME: Again, just like lettuce

BURDOCK
WHEN: Fall the first year, spring the second
HOW TO CONSUME: Cook the root

THREE TO AVOID

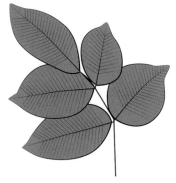

POISON IVY
WHY TO AVOID: It causes dermatitis—itchy skin and blisters

POISON HEMLOCK
WHY TO AVOID: Consuming the root can kill you, like it did Socrates

POISON SUMAC
WHY TO AVOID: Same reason as poison ivy—but even nastier

The Art of Firewood

IT CAN BE SO MUCH MORE THAN CHOPPING AND SPLITTING.

BY C. J. CHIVERS

ON A CRISP DECEMBER DAWN, after a cup of hot coffee and a plate of warm eggs, a winter's weekend routine began. I rousted the kids, who groaned and briefly resisted. While waiting for them to dress and find their way downstairs, I stepped out to the chilly shack and checked the tools and safety kit—padded earmuffs, impact-resistant goggles, heavy gloves, scrench, wedges, rope, first-aid box, and a freshly sharpened spare chain. The saw, a 70.7-cc Husqvarna, brimmed with bar oil and fresh 50:1 fuel.

I walked down the gentle slope behind our house. At the small woodlot at the edge of our neighbor's property were three trees that needed to come down. One, a huge locust, had split almost from the ground to 20 feet up. It swayed and creaked in a light breeze.

Beside the locust was a thick maple that was succumbing to the unrelenting industry of carpenter ants, which had softened a wide band from about five feet above the soil to more than 15 feet overhead. Heart rot had followed the ants' intrusion, leaving much of the trunk as soft as Styrofoam. Without an intervention, this tree was going to meet a violent and unpredictable end. Another ant colony had settled into a second maple nearby. Weakened, that tree leaned precariously over a shed. These were problems that were not going to solve themselves. Our neighbors had invited us to remove the trees and keep whatever firewood we wished.

Soon the kids had joined me and we set to work on a labor that would last, off and on, into spring: felling, limbing, bucking, and then hand-carrying the wood home, where it would be split and then stacked for seasoning. We would do it piecemeal, a few hours at a time, working in the effort between their homework and other demands.

We began by clearing a few bits of brush under the first tree, making a safe place to work and an open escape route in case of the unforeseen. We chose the felling direction and discussed the spots for notch and felling cuts.

The children backed off before the two-stroke engine roared to life. I released the brake. The chain began to spin. A long chore that I would look forward to each weekend had started—harvesting future heat, together, and almost for free.

In an age when many Americans heat with gas, oil, or electricity, the richness and rituals of gathering and seasoning wood for homes risk fading into our past. Those who use wood heat do more than save money, live locally, and keep some of their cash from flowing offshore. They tap into a primal activity and often enjoy rewards beyond what they might expect.

What can I mean? The varied tasks related to heating a home with firewood can create an intimacy with your surroundings and with your family that is as sustaining as the warmth the wood provides as it burns.

Even the woodpiles themselves become a tangible library of memory. Each section of our stack tells of its source. The once bright yellow splits now slowly dulling to brown came from an old locust that had snapped in a hurricane. The rich gray section with heavy bark has its origins in a leader off a massive, trident-shaped oak that crashed to the ground after a heavy, wet snow. That oak piece—my kids named it the beached whale—had to be hand-split in place and carried uphill, chunk by chunk, to the pickup,

> **In an age when many Americans heat with gas, oil, or electricity, the richness and rituals of gathering and seasoning wood for homes risk fading into our past.**

excepting what the kids ferried home in a hand-pulled sled.

Firewood comes to us opportunistically. A neighbor will want a tree felled. A storm will blow through and knock down limbs or uproot and topple entire trees. A few trees will have to go to make way for a home addition or access to a new lot. Sometimes it almost seems as if the wood finds us.

Occasionally the wood can carry other meanings. We cut and carted away the white birch rounds from the sprawling grounds of a condo association at the request of a friend who was managing the place. The property had lost trees in a storm, but the contractor hired to clean up the mess had left much of the wood behind. My children and I ended up with the bounty, glad to help, grateful for the fuel. Not long after we split and stacked a few truckloads, our friend was diagnosed with cancer. She passed with startling speed. Every time we bring a sack of birch inside for the stove, we think of her, aware of the emotional power a wood stack can hold.

Under the trees on that cold December day, the work took its shape. We felled the first maple, then the locust, limbed much of them, and started to carry home the rounds, armload by armload. This would take a long time. But we had been lucky not to have a barrage of winter storms, and we knew we should collect and move as much as we could before winter bore down and covered the site in snow, locking the wood in ice.

The next weekend we returned. And then again, until the wood was frozen up tight. Still, we had plenty to do. Until recently, a weathered stockade fence stood along our southern property line. A previous owner had installed it, and for a few years it had been sagging. Then came Superstorm Sandy in 2012, which neatly snapped a few of the rotting posts at the ground on the way to blowing down several sections of fence.

This led to an epiphany. Why pay the lumber costs for a new fence? Why even replace the fence with a fence? What if, instead of rebuilding a suburban standby, we built a wood-seasoning rack along the property line that would provide the same function—privacy and a wind-break—for a portion of the cost but would be far sturdier, more handsome, and useful, too?

I was busy with work but scrounged the hours to remove what remained of the old stockade. Then I paid a carpenter friend to install a basic rack made with paired pressure-treated 4 x 6s as posts and 2 x 6s running low and parallel to the ground, like baseboards.

A crude but eminently sturdy and functional system had taken form. Each section held more than a half cord. With nine sections and a southern exposure, our would-be fence amply stored (and cured) a sizable portion of our annual firewood needs while taking up almost no yard space. And it looked good.

With time, however, flaws in its quick design emerged. First the posts heaved ever so slightly during seasonal freezes and thaws, forcing the racks out of their original parallel arrangement. This not only looked bad but it also changed the way the firewood sat, so much so that one stack between the posts bulged and collapsed in another hard storm.

Five Ways to Improve Your Firewood

1. Stack wood in a single row, out of the shade, with enough space between the pieces to allow air to pass through. This exposes more wood to sunlight and breeze, which helps dry it out faster.

2. When stacking use a crisscross pattern to make pillars at each end for stability. They act as bookends for the wood in the center.

3. Before splitting wood on a stump, secure an old tire to the top of the stump. After you split the wood, it will lean against the tire instead of falling to the ground.

4. Cut cords shorter than you think (around 14 inches long), split them smaller than you think (three to six inches wide), and vary the size of the splits. The logs will be easier to carry and the fire will be easier to build.

5. Check your state's policies on cutting your own firewood. Many states provide licenses for a nominal fee, or even free, that permit people to remove trees from state land.

Restacking is labor lost. So as the last of the seasoned firewood found its way into our pair of woodstoves, and as we found a new source for wood but could not work with it until a thorough thaw, it was time for an upgrade.

Using level, heavy bar clamps and a come-along for tension and framing lumber to force the posts back square and true, we straightened the posts, bringing each perpendicular to the ground and parallel to the others. These we locked in place with newly purchased pressure-treated 2 x 6s about three feet above the original bottom rack, each resting on a cleat for extra support. In one rack we framed the opening for a small gate.

When winter loosened its grip, we returned to the trees at the edge of the woodlot out back and finished cleaning them up. Our neighbors lent us their John Deere 52 log splitter, a minibeast and a gem from the early 1980s that had become slightly balky with age. We commenced the next step: splitting the gathered fuel to size.

After a few shifts I managed to break the pull cord off the starter. A call to a friend who repairs commercial fishing boats led to a quick session in the yard, during which we removed the starter, rethreaded and tied in the cord, and then cleaned and tuned the carburetor. Soon the machine was purring, its old Briggs & Stratton engine contentedly revived. Over the course of the next few weekends my sons and I converted about 10 cords of green wood into splits.

By then spring had warmed the yard. Potatoes were sprouting and asparagus, too. The woodstoves in the house and the shack were clean and silent, idle until fall. The new green firewood was neatly piled about the property, beginning to dry. The chainsaw was cleaned and ready to be put up for the warm season with a fresh tank of high-octane, no-ethanol fuel.

We were done. And we knew the satisfying feeling of being, in one area at least, well-prepared by our own sweat and our own hands. My only regret was that it was over. We'd have to wait another year to resume.

Chivers's son splits wood during a recent winter.

How to Fell a Tree with an Ax

A tree comes down in three cuts.

CUT ONE:

At a 45-degree angle downward

CUT TWO:

At a 45-degree angle upward, to intersect with the first cut

CUT THREE:

Into the opposite side of the tree, parallel to the ground. It should be slightly above or equal to the point of the notch formed by cuts one and two. Stop when there is a hinge left that's about 10 percent of the width of the tree. Pound a felling wedge into the cut and the tree should fall away from you.

How to Split Firewood

NOT EVERY HOBBY CAN BE LEARNED IN A MONTH, A YEAR, OR EVEN A DECADE. SOME ARE THE BLUEPRINTS TO EVERY SKILL YOU'LL EVER LEARN.

SEASONED SPLITTERS USE a maul, not an ax, to prep firewood. (With its slim taper, an ax head often gets stuck in the end grain.) Don't use a chopping block—it reduces the arc of the swing, which decreases power. Instead, place the log on the ground, five inches closer than the length of the maul handle. Stand with your feet shoulder-width apart; place your dominant hand at the bottom of the handle and the other hand three-quarters up the handle. Rest the maul on the wood, then lift it all the way up—your bottom arm should be straight and your top arm slightly bent. As you begin the downward motion, slide your top hand down to your bottom hand. Use your whole body, not just your arms, and bend your knees slightly, snapping them back a split second before hitting the wood. "You want to drive the maul through the wood, so complete the swing once you make contact," says Nathan Waterfield (pictured), owner of Timberworks Forest Management & Specialty Works in Cherry Valley, New York.

Signs Your Wood Is Well-Seasoned

Wood needs to age, or *season,* before it will burn well.

It doesn't smell like wood. Most of the woody scent you get is caused by moisture.

It's dull in color. Seasoned wood should look gray.

It's not heavy. Water makes up as much as three-quarters of the weight of a green piece of wood.

The ends have cracks. As the wood dries out, it becomes more brittle.

The bark is missing or comes off easily. When the moisture goes, the bark usually goes with it.

It sounds hollow when you hit it against something. (Probably best if that something is another log.)

STRATEGY:
HOW TO FORAGE FOR FIREWOOD

1. Wood from spruce, aspen, birch, willow, or pine trees makes good kindling. It lights easily.
2. Be wary of wood that you find on the ground as it's more likely to be wet or rotten.
3. Most of your campfire wood should come from low branches. If they snap off easily,

they're dead already and will burn well.
4. For longer-burning wood, find a nut-bearing tree. Oak, hickory, walnut, and maple are all hardwoods, which means they're denser and have a higher heat content, measured in British thermal units (BTUs).

HEAT CONTENT BY TYPE OF WOOD

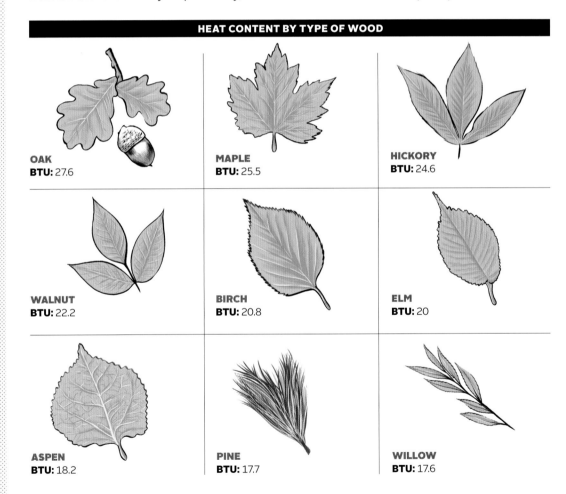

OAK
BTU: 27.6

MAPLE
BTU: 25.5

HICKORY
BTU: 24.6

WALNUT
BTU: 22.2

BIRCH
BTU: 20.8

ELM
BTU: 20

ASPEN
BTU: 18.2

PINE
BTU: 17.7

WILLOW
BTU: 17.6

Three Tree Cuts Everyone Should Know

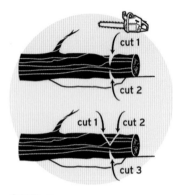

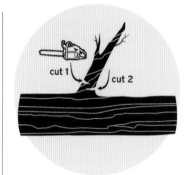

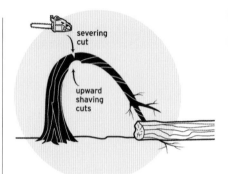

CUT 1
NOTCH AND FOLD

A felled tree usually has saw-pinching areas where the top of the log is under compression and the bottom is under tension. If you have access to the top and bottom of the log, you can handle this one of two ways. Make a cut straight down from the top and finish by cutting up from the bottom. The problem is the saw can get pinched in the down cut. Another option is to make an angled cut through about a third of the log's diameter. Make a second angled cut that intersects the first. Remove the wedge. Make a third cut up from the bottom that intersects the point of the wedge.

CUT 2
OFFSET CUT AND SNAP

Limbing a tree can leave a mass of brush underfoot that can trip you up. Here's a method to have more control over the cleanup. For relatively small branches, up to three inches in diameter, say, cut them in a way that allows you to snap them off cleanly by hand and toss them to the side. Make two offset cuts, one on each side of the branch. Each cut goes slightly past the branch's center. Do a bunch of limbs that way, put the saw down, snap each one off, and toss it into a pile, away from where you're working.

CUT 3
SPRING POLE RELEASE

A falling tree will often bend a sapling or a branch under it, leaving you with what's called a spring pole. Catapult would be a better name. The bent branch or sapling contains a tremendous amount of stored energy. If you crosscut its fibers, you release that energy—just like you released the rope on a catapult. To deal with this safely, make a series of parallel cuts on the inside (compression side) of the spring pole, shaving down its wood. Make a small vertical cut on top, but don't sever the branch. The pole should release slowly on its own.

THE STANCE

When the bottom of a chain-saw bar makes contact with a log, it pulls you toward the log. When the top of a bar makes contact, it pushes you away. If you're not prepared for either, you can get knocked onto your butt. So use the boxer's stance. For a right-handed person, that means standing with your left foot forward and your right foot back. Bend your knees as you pivot the saw through the log, and think about where the saw will exit. You don't want to swing out of the cut, across the toe of your boot, and into your leg.

ESSENTIAL GEAR

BECAUSE YOU'LL NOT ONLY LOOK THE PART BUT BE SAFE, TOO.

Tall logging boots provide ankle support and traction when the going gets tough. You can cut safely only if you can stand firmly (see "The Stance," above).

Chainsaw chaps are a must. If you cut into your leg, their chain-stopping fabric snarls the saw's clutch before the chain can do real damage.

A forestry helmet protects your eyes, ears, and head. It feels confining at first, but you'll be glad you have it on when you get swatted in the face by a falling branch.

Cold-weather logging gloves with chain-stopping fabric are important for the same reason that chaps are.

A cant hook is a time-honored tool for turning and positioning logs. Your back will thank you.

A Skill for a Lifetime: Fishing

BY C. J. CHIVERS

SOME TASKS ARE so rich in their demands that the hope of mastering them leads to the pursuit of others, and then to others, and so on for life.

When pursued with intensity, fishing works like that. Find someone who catches a variety of fish, season after season, year after year, in varied weather, habitats, and conditions, and you have almost certainly found someone who possesses a range of disparate but interlocking abilities. Being an expert caster, while a handsome competency, is nowhere near enough. Just as cats are not predators solely by claw, people who master fishing's main goal—consistently harvesting fish—draw from a fuller set of skills. They can handle and work on boats. They read weather, currents, and tides. They easily tie a multiplicity of knots—in ropes, wire, or line. They understand food webs. And they typically can put to use any number of tools—a cast net, a fillet knife and its sharpening stone, or a miter saw when a dock or boat repair is required. They have forced their abilities to cohere.

This is why, in our house, fishing lies near the center of what my wife and I consider our children's living classroom.

This is not to understate the obvious: At heart, old-school fishing remains about catching and eating fish. The waters near our home provide us a large fraction of our annual protein, beginning with yellow perch caught through ice in winter, continuing with the spring squid run on a nearby oceanic shoal, and then plunging full-bore into successive finfish

ADVICE FROM AN ANGLER:
NEVER RUN OUT OF WORMS

The next time you have a hard time finding worms for fish bait, force the tines of a pitchfork into the ground and twang the handle. This creates vibrations that cause the worms to come up to the surface.

harvests deep into fall, as various saltwater species migrate near New England's shores.

But as our children learn to harvest the bounties that swim within reach, they are developing and honing many other skills, from simple carpentry to animal husbandry to cooking, brining, and pickling. We allow the possibilities to expand. Our gardens and fruit trees are fueled by *fish frames*—the bones and heads of fish with meat removed—buried in compost piles. The trellises and beds the kids helped build provide all manner of food (garlic, potatoes, onions, leeks, beans, squash, and tomatoes) that we serve with the fish. The turkeys and chickens the kids raise eat with delight any excess bait.

And always it is back to the sea, where each trip helps the children develop a sense of self-reliance and achievement. One weeknight last summer we were about 15 miles out, tending the bottom in a rocky rip on a tide that had been dumping against a stiff wind. An ocean swell had been pounding across it all, creating a confused washtub sea. Once we had fish in the cooler, the crossing back to the mainland was black, and it bisected a shipping lane that required attention at the helm. (The boys, 12 and 14, pointed out the navigation lights on a tug towing a barge, determined its relative direction, and called out "all clear" on the course we had chosen.) Then, as we approached land, a blackout knocked out shoreline power, leaving little to navigate by as the hull covered the last stretch.

The boys hardly noticed. They spotted the seawall opening by scanning along a compass heading, then readied lines as we puttered up the channel past darkened docks before scooting cross-tide into the last tight passage. There they sprung from the gunwale to the dock to tie the boat off. I cut the engines and listened as they continued the work.

The next morning the two of them carried the heavy cooler from the pickup to the cleaning table, retrieved fish from the ice, and broke out the knives. An hour or so later they had filleted the catch and buried the frames in compost beside the strawberry beds. Mick, who likes to cook, was talking recipes. Jack helped me think through the design and placement of a new block and tackle.

Everything about the rhythm we had fallen into showed that the old saw—give a man a fish and he will eat for a day, but teach him to fish and he will eat for a lifetime—only brushes the truth.

Teach your daughter to fish and she may become a biologist, a mechanic, a deckhand, a carpenter, and an artist, all on her spare time. You may find that you have a child who can free-dive with a spear or build you a meticulously shingled storage shed with a classically pitched roof for your gear and lobster pots. And you will have fish, plenty to eat and plenty to share—an abundance of the food that propelled you all into motion in the first place but required that you learn many other skills to succeed.

ADVICE FROM AN ANGLER:
TEMPT MORE TROUT

Even in the most heavily fished streams, trout find it difficult to resist a worm offered in either of the following two ways. One successful method utilizes a twig with a leaf or two attached. After the worm-baited hook is pushed through the edge of the leaf, the twig is allowed to float downstream. When the leaf drifts over a likely pool, the hook is jerked free by a twitch of the rod tip. The bait then sinks slowly to the bottom, coaxing the trout into striking. The other method is to mold a ball of clay or mud over the worm and hook. The ball is lowered slowly into the water and washes away to expose the worm.

The Ultimate Survival Dog

DURING THE GOOD TIMES, the preapocalypse, you want a dog that's loyal, smart, and obedient. You also want a dog that barks like hell when a stranger walks up your driveway. The German shorthaired pointer (pictured) has these qualities and a lot more. The breed has pulled sleds, carried packs, and gone into battle with elite U.S. forces. Its webbed paws make it a good swimmer. It can be trained to retrieve game that you kill—or to kill small animals itself. The dog's versatility derives from deliberate breeding: Spanish and English pointers, the dalmatian, the vizsla, and a tracking hound all went into making this crafty canine. Its complex ancestry also makes it susceptible to few ailments and likely to live up to 14 years. So maybe stock up on dog food, too.

STRATEGY:
HOW TO IDENTIFY TRACKS

WHETHER YOU'RE FINDING FOOD OR AVOIDING POSSIBLE PREDATORS, YOU SHOULD KNOW HOW TO RECOGNIZE THE DIFFERENT PRINTS ANIMALS LEAVE.

DOG
Not to be confused with a coyote: more oblong with less prominent claws and a smaller hind footprint

DEER
A walking deer leaves a print like this one. A running deer's toes spread at the top and look more like an upward V.

TURKEY
Tracks can be as big as 5 inches wide, with three long front toes. A small one in the back occasionally shows up.

BLACK BEAR
Similar to grizzly bear prints, but smaller and with shorter claws

SKUNK
The hind foot appears similar to human feet, with claws that rarely leave an impression.

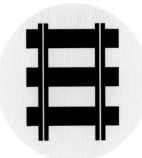

TRAIN
Easy to spot and follow. Don't get too close.

How to Paddle a Kayak

THERE ARE THREE BASIC STROKES TO GET YOU ANYWHERE YOU NEED TO GO ON THE RIVER.

FORWARD/BACKWARD STROKE

CONTROLS FORWARD AND BACKWARD MOVEMENT

1. Reach forward with the paddle blade and submerge it completely in the water—but not so deep that your hand goes in.

2. Pull the blade straight back, parallel to your boat. The blade should be close enough to almost touch the kayak.

3. Switch sides and repeat. (Reverse the stroke to go backward.)

SWEEP STROKE

TURNS THE FRONT OR BACK OF THE KAYAK

1. Reach forward with the paddle blade opposite the side you want the boat to move. For example, if you'd like to turn right, reach forward with your left paddle blade.

2. Put the blade in the water and sweep it outward, arcing away from the front of the boat.

3. Repeat on the same side until the boat is aimed where you want it.

DRAW

MOVES YOUR KAYAK LATERALLY WITHOUT CHANGING DIRECTION

1. Reach out in the direction you want to move the boat and place your paddle in the water, directly to the side of your hip.

2. Pull the water in toward you, as if pushing it under your seat.

3. Continue as needed.

How to Paddle a Canoe

ACCORDING TO ALEX Comb of Stewart River Boatworks in Knife River, Minnesota, who started building wood and canvas canoes in early adulthood, the first step in paddling a canoe is selecting a properly sized paddle. With your hands above your head in the surrender position, the distance between the pinkie edges of your palms should be just shy of the distance from the top of the paddle to the blade.

1. Holding the paddle with one hand on the handle and the other just above the blade, sit up straight and lean slightly forward. Dip the paddle into the water with the blade at a slight angle to the direction of travel.

2. Pull the blade perpendicular to the hull as it enters the water. Pull back, finishing the stroke as the paddle passes your hip.

3. If you don't want to turn away from the side you're paddling on, adjust the paddle parallel to the hull at the end of your stroke and press outward. This is called a J stroke.

Budapest, Hungary, June 19, 2015. Participants weigh a self-made canoe made of concrete before their race. In Hungary, this form of sports has existed since 2012. Concrete canoes are the same size as general sporting canoes—most of them weigh around 150kg but some only weigh 40kg—while a plastic composite racing canoe is usually around 20kg.

How to Make a Concrete Canoe

MANY ENGINEERING COMPETITIONS CHALLENGE TEAMS TO MAKE A CANOE OUT OF WHAT SEEMS LIKE AN UNFLOATABLE SUBSTANCE: CONCRETE. HERE'S HOW TO MAKE YOUR OWN WHEN HOLLOWING OUT A TREE NO LONGER CHALLENGES YOU.

STEP 1

Design a basic hull form or use an existing form on a CAD program.

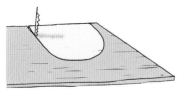

STEP 2

Print cross sections of the hull at regular intervals onto paper templates. Transfer these templates to pieces of plywood.

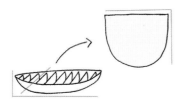

STEP 3

Cut out the cross sections from the plywood using a jigsaw or a band saw.

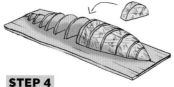

STEP 4

Assemble the plywood pieces by standing them up—spaced according to the design—and fastening them to a rigid piece of lumber called a *strong back*. Insert pieces of rigid foam insulation in the gaps, then trim the excess using a knife or reciprocating saw.

STEP 5

Sight down the hull form to locate any low areas in the foam or plywood. If you find any, build them out with drywall compound. Once any drywall compound is dry, sand the shape as smooth as possible. Apply water with a cloth to the hull form to reduce the concrete's tendency to bond to it.

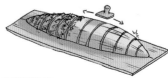

STEP 6

Mix the concrete and apply a ½- to 1-inch layer to the hull using trowels, floats, and your hands. The thicker the layer, the heavier the boat, but also the better the boat will tolerate stress.

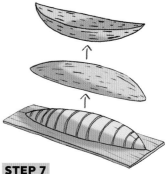

STEP 7

Once the concrete is dry, fill any small blemishes, then let it dry again and sand it smooth. Once the smoothing is complete, carefully lift the hull from the mold.

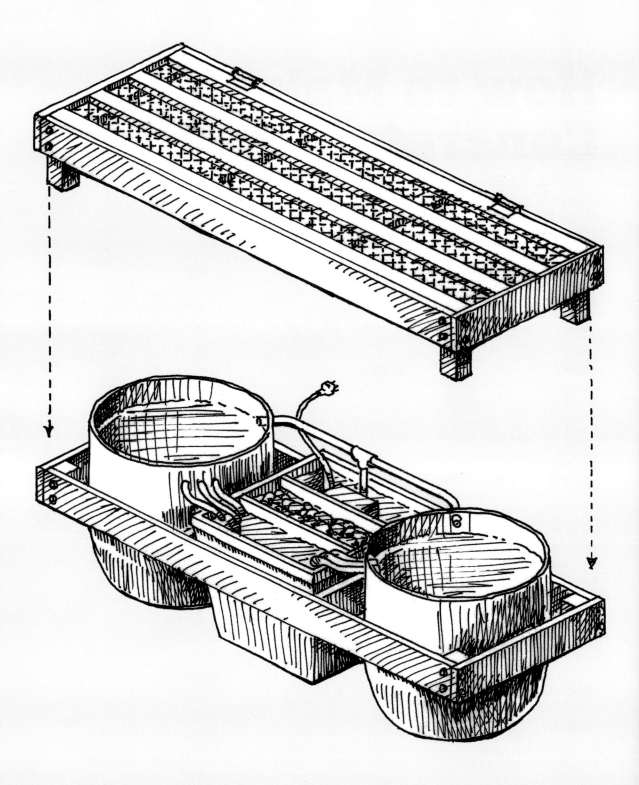

How to Make a Bait Barrel

USING FOUND SUPPLIES AND A FEW BASICS FROM THE HARDWARE STORE, WE
BUILT A LIVE BAITWELL FOR A SEASON OF FISHING IN THE LAKE BEHIND OUR HOUSE.

BY C. J. CHIVERS

AS LONGER DAYS and rising temperatures warmed the lake behind our house this spring and the lake's fish, frogs, and reptiles gathered in the nearest cove, three of my boys began scouring the shallows for prey, using dip nets and minnow traps to capture all manner of life. Soon they had an assortment of creatures in aquariums in one of their bedrooms and a proposal for their parents to consider: Can we build large outdoor tanks to keep bait alive and ready for fishing season? The lake's largemouth bass and pickerel, they said, would be more likely to strike fish from their own habitat—bait that also happens to be free.

The idea had merit, as long as costs could be contained. And so we took it on.

Mick, who is 14, did the planning. First he took stock of what was already available at home or on our next-door neighbors' property—a pair of plastic lobster-bait barrels that we had picked up over the years, several old pressure-treated 4 x 4s, an abundance of six-foot slats from a fallen cedar fence, a rectangular plastic basin about 16 inches deep, boxes of varied fasteners, a slightly bent roll of galvanized wire mesh, about four feet of white polymer trim board, and a small pile of 30-inch lichen-encrusted drops from a dock built years ago with composite deck boards.

He then set to sketching a design and compiling a list of what we would need to finish the job. His plan called for shortening the height of the barrels and securing them in a simple wooden-and-composite-board frame. The rectangular basin would be seated between them. It would be divided into three chambers and serve as the system's heart. One chamber would receive outflow from the bait barrels, another would be filled with gravel for filtering, and a third would house a pump, which would send freshly filtered water back into the two barrels via hoses joined at a T-junction. The system would run in a figure-eight loop, with the pump powered by an outdoor outlet at a tool shed, next to which the apparatus would be built. I offered one modification: Why not place a portion of the tanks below grade, in the cooler earth, to keep the water from overheating on hot days? My wife required another: a child-safe top.

To complete such a system, we bought several items from the lumberyard and pet-supply store—a pair of pressure-treated studs (rated for ground contact), a bag of clean gravel, a 500-gallons-per-hour electric pump, and a tube of aquarium-grade silicone. A stop in the plumbing aisle yielded hoses and fittings to connect it all together.

The early stages of the project went smoothly. I trust Mick with tools, and he knows how to

use many of them quite well. With a jigsaw he reduced the barrel heights, then measured their diameters, and with the miter saw cut pieces of pressure-treated studs for a frame. The dock drops were refashioned as side braces that matched the barrels' contours, holding things snug. Next he cut the composite trim board into panels to divide the basin's interior. Once he secured them with silicone, the filter was in place, with gravel in the center compartment.

The work became trickier as Mick shifted to the plumbing. In a perfect world everything would fit and be level, allowing the pump and gravity to work in practice as they had in design. But as we dug the holes where the tanks would sit, we were surprised by what we should have expected: a thick tree root. This caused one tank to sit, higher than the other. The plumbing holes were no longer level with each other. An afternoon of jury-rigging ensued as we cut fresh drainage with a hole saw and tinkered with hose lengths and placement until the flow into the barrels was equalized. We added another pair of drainage pipes to achieve equilibrium between the pump and the barrels' drainage. Water flowing out now matched water flowing in—an important point, or the center basin would end up dry and the pump dead.

The child-safe top was formed by making a lattice with fence slats, which sandwiched the wire mesh, and then building a 2 x 6 pressure-treated frame that stood on post legs just above the height of the tanks. A pair of aged door hinges provided the last touch, allowing the lattice lid to be opened and closed like the lid on a huge cooler. This would do more than stop small children; it would discourage thieving raccoons.

Our bait tanks were done, ready for use.

The next day, when I checked on the pump, I saw the first fish swimming inside, along with a painted turtle. The boys had already been busy.

How to Make a Turkey Call

THE SLATE-AND-STRIKER IS the simplest turkey call to create and very effective. Champion call maker Don Bald, of Lebanon, Illinois, starts by cutting a piece of slate (he uses chalkboard he salvaged from a school wrecked by a tornado) with a band saw and smoothing out the edges with fine-grit sandpaper. The piece should be $1/8$-inch thick and fit comfortably in the palm of your hand.

The striker consists of a handle and peg. Use oak or another hardwood for the peg. Bald turns his pegs on a lathe, making them just under $1/2$ inch in diameter at the top and gently tapered down to the tip, which he rounds off like the business end of a pool cue. All you need for the handle is a piece of dried corncob. Just drill a hole, place some epoxy and the striker in the hole, and test it out. The shorter the striker, the higher-pitched the sound, so give the slate a few strikes, adjusting the length of the peg below the handle until you get the pitch you want. Then let the epoxy set.

Before you use the call, rub both the slate and the striker with 280-grit sandpaper. It's like chalking the cue, and it'll give you a better sound.

GETTING STARTED IN:

Canning and Pickling

IT'S DELICIOUS AND HEALTHY. WHAT ARE YOU WAITING FOR?

FOR MOST OF HUMAN HISTORY, preservation was a survival mechanism. Fermenting and pickling, among the oldest forms of cooking we know, kept us from getting sick. Over millennia, we developed simple, almost instinctual techniques as varied as the cultures that span the globe. But in only a couple hundred years, technology has reduced the repertoire of most people to two—refrigeration and buying commercially processed foods. And in forgoing the time-consuming tasks we once used to maximize our harvest, we've abandoned two fundamentals of eating: nutrition and flavor.

Medical studies are now proving what our instincts said all along: Good bacteria and microbes are essential to our health. Preserving food by fermenting is the easiest way to get them into our bodies since it allows bacteria to multiply and grow before entering our gut. And if you've ever tasted a perfect kimchi, you know it's got a funky, sour flavor unlike anything else.

So after generations of consuming industrialized food, let's reintroduce a practice as old as agriculture itself. No culinary training is necessary, and the results taste better than anything you can buy in a store. Sure, it takes some new equipment, patience, and discipline. Don't sweat the learning curve. Unlike our ancestors, we aren't preserving because we have to, but simply because we want to.

FERMENTING VS. PICKLING

Pickling simply refers to the practice of preserving food in an acidic medium. Fermenting is a type of pickling, because the salty brine and lactobacilli create their own acidic environment. So while this recipe uses fermentation, you can pickle things (including cucumbers) simply by submerging them in vinegar and refrigerating them. They will still taste great but won't include the cohort of healthy bacteria.

WHEN YOU SHOULD CAN

No one wants to eat green beans for three weeks straight. Use boiling water to kill bacteria and vacuum-seal your excess harvest in a mason jar and you won't have to—it'll stay good for up to a year.

FOODS

The extra fruits and vegetables from your garden are a great place to start. Avoid anything with bruises or mold and try to preserve fruits and vegetables as soon as possible after they've been harvested. Depending on the produce, you'll usually get one quart canned for every three to four pounds of fresh produce.

WHAT TO EXPECT

TIME

The actual *canning*—sterilizing airtight containers in hot water—usually takes only about half an hour. But you'll want to set aside a whole afternoon to make time for food prep and the fact that you have to process in batches since most pots won't hold very many jars at once.

EQUIPMENT

GLASS MASON JARS
The easiest to find are Ball or Kerr

JAR LIDS AND BANDS
Sealing metal discs and the threaded metal rings that hold them down

OVEN MITT

CANNING RACK

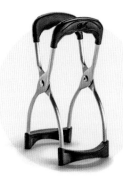

JAR LIFTER WITH RUBBER GRIPS

LARGE POT

RECIPES

There is a canning bible, and it's called *Ball Complete Book of Home Preserving*. It's been around in one form or another since 1909, so its recipes are time-tested. Most importantly, each recipe explains how to prepare a food before canning it, which might be as simple as heating whole fruit but often requires a bit of cooking.

PROCESS

First—yes, canning actually means sealing food in jars. Once you've got the food packed, you can can it two ways—either with a big pot of boiling water or a pressure canner, which gets even hotter. High-acid foods, like fruits and salsa, are safe to process in a pot because the acidity does some of the work of killing bacteria. That makes jellies and jams the easiest place to start. Low-acid foods need to be processed in a pressure canner. The processes follow the same steps, though: Mason jars are warmed in the hot water and then packed, leaving a little bit of space to create a strong vacuum seal. The filled jar goes back into the hot water for as long as the recipe says. Then you wait for the characteristic popping sound made as the jar cools and the vacuum secures the lid.

WHY CANNING WORKS
(AND HOW TO MAKE SURE IT DID)

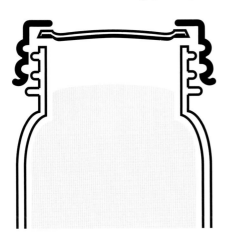

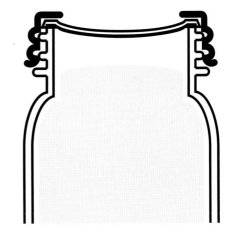

1. Jar lids have a ring of a compound called Plastisol around the edge in a trough that fits over the top of the jar. Plastisol is soft at high temperatures but hardens at room temperature. As the heat of the canning process causes gases and the food to expand, creating higher pressure inside the jar than outside, air is able to vent out through the Plastisol.

2. Then, when the jar cools, the Plastisol hardens into a tight seal. By the time the jar has cooled to room temperature, so much air has vented that pressure inside the jar is lower than outside. This makes the properly sealed lid concave—if it's flat or bulging, it's not sealed. Test it by tapping the lid—a pinging sound means a proper seal.

WHEN YOU SHOULD PICKLE

If you want to improve upon nature even more, submerging foods in an acidic environment not only preserves them for up to three or four months but also gives them a distinctive tangy flavor.

FOODS

You can pickle just about anything, but if you're fermenting—a type of pickling—use produce with a high water content, like root vegetables, cabbage, kale, or cucumbers. Fruits will ferment, but because yeast feast on their sugars, you may need a starter like kombucha or extra salt to prevent them from spoiling or becoming too alcoholic.

WHAT TO EXPECT

TIME

Patience is key. You won't spend hours in the kitchen, but, depending on the method of pickling you choose, it can take anywhere from a day to weeks to achieve the perfect flavor. Feel free to eat your pickles as quickly as you want, though.

EQUIPMENT

GLASS, PORCELAIN, OR CERAMIC CONTAINER

PICKLING SALT

STONE OR OTHER WEIGHT

MIXING BOWL

WOODEN SPOON

CHEESECLOTH

RECIPES

The *Ball Complete Book of Home Preserving* also offers expert guidance on pickles. So do we: Try the Classic Dill Pickle recipe below.

PROCESS

Pickles are just produce on acid—either vinegar or fermentation's lactic acid. Adding vinegar, salt, sugar, and spices in a jar creates a quick pickle in as little as 24 hours. Fermentation takes longer because it has two stages. The salt in the vinegar mix draws water out of the cucumbers, forming a brine that makes it harder for harmful bacteria to grow. Then good lactobacilli bacteria already living on the cucumbers convert sugars into lactic acid, which preserves the produce and adds tanginess. A clean cloth or cheesecloth secured with a rubber band vents gases from fermentation and forms a barrier to mold and harmful bacteria. After a couple weeks in the jar, fermented pickles are ready.

RECIPE:

The Classic Dill Pickle

INGREDIENTS
(For a one-gallon container)

4 lb	4-inch pickling cucumbers
2 tbsp	dill seed or 4-5 heads fresh or dry dill weed
1/2 cup	noniodized salt
1/4 cup	distilled white vinegar
8 cups	water

1. Wash cucumbers and remove blossom ends, leaving ¼ inch of stem attached.
2. Place half the dill at the bottom of your container, then the cucumbers, then the remaining dill.
3. In a separate bowl, mix salt, vinegar, and water until salt dissolves.
4. Pour mixture over cucumbers, put a weight on top to keep them submerged, then tightly cover the container with cheesecloth.
5. Check the container several times a week and promptly remove surface scum or mold. Pickles that are soft, slimy, or excessively smelly should be discarded.
6. At room temperature, expect to allow three to four weeks of fermentation (choosing when to stop is a matter of taste). Lower temperatures slow the process; temperatures above 80° will make the pickles too soft.

With thanks to Benjamin Chapman and the National Center for Home Food Preservation

How to Pitch a Tent

PARKER LIAUTAUD,
POLAR ADVENTURER

When four-time polar explorer Parker Liautaud embarked on his first trip to the North Pole at 15, he'd never pitched a tent before. "I only learned to set up the tent when I saw it for the first time, which was when I got to Norway," he says. Liautaud has learned a lot since then. Every tent is different, so the biggest thing, he says, is to practice. You should be completely familiar with all of your equipment before you ever use it in a real situation.

1. Choose your ground wisely. Of course you don't want to sleep on lava rock, but even little bumps can make your tent floor uncomfortable. If your tent is long, position it so that the narrowest part faces the wind. Otherwise the broad side will act like a sail, which could lead to a collapse.

2. When you take the tent out of its pack, don't lose or ignore any piece. Even a lost clip could mean a less structurally secure lodging. When you place the spikes, make sure the ground is solid. Placing them at a slight angle also helps keep the rope or tent holes from slipping off.

Placing your tent on a slight incline will keep water from gathering under you if it rains.

How to Build a Campfire

TWO BOY SCOUT–
APPROVED METHODS

THE LOG CABIN

Good For: Campfire cooking, slow-burning fires

How To: Lay your wood crisscross in a square, the way you did with Lincoln Logs as a kid, around your tinder and kindling. Use larger pieces of wood as the base and work up from there, with the smallest pieces at the top.

THE TEPEE

Good For: Hot fires, windy conditions

How To: Stand up three or four big sticks so they form a point over your bundle of kindling. They act as a chimney, drawing air in. Then add your larger logs in the same shape around the existing structure for support.

3.

Threat: Medium

THINGS HAVE GONE WRONG. THERE'S A CHANCE YOU'LL HAVE TO ABANDON YOUR HOME AND HEAD FOR SAFER TERRITORY. THE NEIGHBORS NO LONGER OPEN THEIR DOORS WHEN YOU KNOCK.

How Not to Die

AT LEAST NOT TODAY.

ACCIDENTS ARE THE leading cause of death among U.S. men 18 to 50 years old, accounting for 37,000 of roughly 148,000 annual fatalities. Some instances of unintentional death, to use the official term, are unavoidable—wrong place, wrong time—but most aren't. Staying alive requires recognizing danger, feeling fear, and reacting. "We interpret external cues through our subconscious fear centers very quickly," says Harvard University's David Ropeik, author of *How Risky Is It, Really?* Trouble is, even smart, sober, experienced men can fail to register signals of an imminent threat. Here we present 20 easy-to-miss risks and how to avoid or survive them.

OUTSMART WILDLIFE.

If you come face-to-face with a wild animal, the natural response is to bolt, but that can trigger the animal's predatory instinct. On July 6, 2011, Brian Matayoshi, 57, and his wife, Marylyn, 58, were hiking in Yellowstone National Park when they came upon a grizzly bear and fled, screaming. Brian was bitten and clawed to death; Marylyn, who had stopped and crouched behind a tree, was approached by the bear but left unharmed.

STAT: Each year three to five people are killed in North America in wild animal attacks, primarily by sharks and bears.

DO: Avoid shark-infested waters. As for bears,

Pepper spray designed to stop a charging bear can save you, but for Pete's sake, don't wait until the animal is inches from your hand.

always carry repellent pepper spray when hiking; it can stop a charging bear from as much as 30 feet away. To reduce the risk of an attack, give bears a chance to get out of your way. "Try to stay in the open," says Larry Aumiller, manager of Alaska's McNeil River State Game Sanctuary. "If you have to move through thick brush, make noise by clapping and shouting."

DON'T MESS WITH VENDING MACHINES.

You skipped lunch. You need a snack. You insert money into a vending machine, press the buttons, and nothing comes out. You get mad.

STAT: Vending machines caused 37 deaths between 1978 and 1995, crushing customers who rocked and toppled the dispensers. No recent stats exist, but the machines are still a danger.

DON'T: Skip lunch.

➡ STAY ON THE DOCK.

On May 20, 2013, Kyle McGonigle was on a dock on Kentucky's Rough River Lake. A dog swimming nearby yelped, and McGonigle, 36, saw that it was struggling to stay above water. He dove in to save the dog, but both he and the animal drowned, victims of electric-shock drowning (ESD). Cords plugged into an outlet on the dock had slipped into the water and electrified it.

STAT: The number of annual deaths from ESD in the U.S. are unknown since they are counted among all drownings. But anecdotal evidence shows that ESD is widespread. ESD prevention groups have successfully urged some states to enact safety standards, including the installation of ground-fault circuit interrupters and a central shutoff for a dock's electrical system.

DON'T: Swim within 100 yards of any wired dock. But do check whether docks follow safety standards.

KEEP IT ON THE DIRT.

On the morning of July 14, 2013, Taylor Fails, 20, turned left in his 2004 Yamaha Rhino ATV at a paved intersection near his Las Vegas–area home. The high-traction tire treads gripped the road and the vehicle flipped, ejecting Fails and a 22-year-old passenger. Fails died at the scene; the passenger sustained minor injuries.

STAT: One-third of fatal ATV accidents take place on paved roads; more than 300 people died in on-road ATV wrecks in 2011.

DO: Ride only off-road. Paul Vitrano, executive vice president of the ATV Safety Institute, says, "Soft, knobby tires are designed for traction on uneven ground and will behave unpredictably on pavement." In some cases, tires will grip enough to cause an ATV to flip, as in the Nevada incident. "If you must cross a paved road to continue on an approved trail, go straight across in first gear."

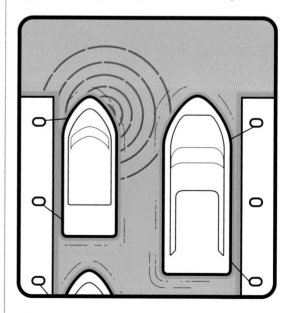

Dockside water can become electrified by a short in an onboard appliance, a faulty wire connecting a boat to the dock's power outlet, or exposed wiring in the dock's power source. The current courses through a swimmer's body and can lead to electric-shock drowning.

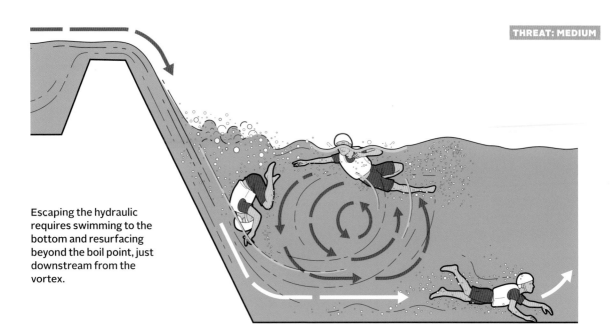

Escaping the hydraulic requires swimming to the bottom and resurfacing beyond the boil point, just downstream from the vortex.

⬆ BEWARE LOW-HEAD DAMS.

Found on small or moderate-size streams and rivers, low-head dams are used to regulate water flow or prevent invasive species from swimming upstream. But watch out. "They're called drowning machines because they could not be designed better to drown people," says Kevin Colburn of American Whitewater, a nonprofit whitewater preservation group. To a boater heading downstream, the dams look like a line of flat reflective water. But water rushing over the dam creates a spinning cylinder of water that can trap a capsized boater.

STAT: Eight to 12 people a year die in low-head and other dam-related whitewater accidents.

DO: Curl up, drop to the bottom, and move downstream if caught in a hydraulic. "It's a counterintuitive thing to do, but the only outflow is at the bottom," Colburn says. Surface only after you've cleared the vortex near the dam.

MOW ON THE LEVEL.

Whirring blades are the obvious hazard. But most lawn mower–related deaths result from riding mowers flipping over on a slope and crushing the drivers.

STAT: About 95 Americans are killed by riding mowers each year.

DO: Mow up and down a slope, not sideways along it. How steep is too steep? "If you can't back up a slope, do not mow on it," Carl Purvis of the U.S. Consumer Product Safety Commission advises.

DON'T HOLD YOUR BREATH.

If you want to take a long swim underwater, the trick is to breathe in and out a few times and take a big gulp of air before you submerge. Right? Dead wrong. Hyperventilating not only doesn't increase the oxygen in your blood, it also decreases the amount of CO_2, the compound that informs the brain of the need to breathe. Without that natural signal, you may hold your breath until you pass out and drown. This is known as shallow-water blackout.

STAT: Drowning is the fifth largest cause of accidental death in the U.S., claiming about 10 lives a day. No one knows how many of these are due to shallow-water blackout, but its prevalence has led to the formation of advocacy groups, such as Shallow Water Blackout Prevention.

DON'T: Hyperventilate before swimming underwater and don't push yourself to stay submerged as long as possible.

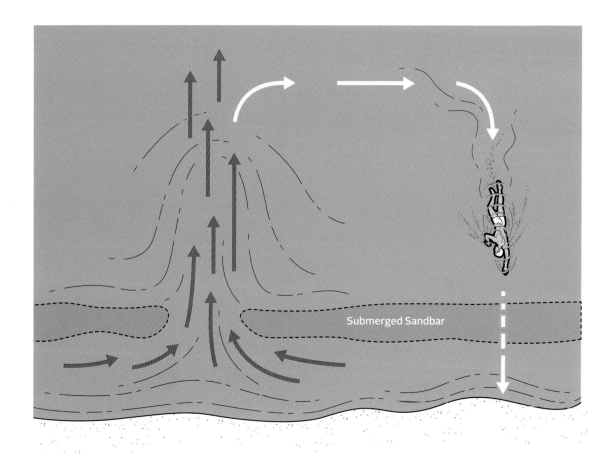

Submerged Sandbar

GO WITH THE FLOW.

The tourist season got off to a grisly start in 2013 in Gulf Shores, Alabama. During a two-day period in early June, four men drowned after being caught in rip currents. The unusually strong currents were invisible, not even roiling the surface. Rip currents occur when water rushing back from the shoreline is channeled through a narrow gap between two sand bars, accelerating the outward flow.

STAT: More than 100 Americans drown in rip currents each year.

DO: Allow the current to carry you out beyond the riptide's flow, then swim laterally until you reach a position where you can turn and stroke safely to shore.

⬆ FORD CAREFULLY.

A shallow stream can pack a surprising amount of force, making fording extremely dangerous. Once you've been knocked off your feet, you can get dragged down by the weight of your gear, strike rocks in the water, or succumb to hypothermia.

STAT: Water-related deaths outnumber all other fatalities in U.S. national parks; no specific statistics are available for accidents while fording streams.

DO: Cross at a straight, wide section of water. Toss a stick into the current; if it moves faster than a walking pace, don't cross. Unhitch waist and sternum fasteners before crossing—a wet pack can pull you under.

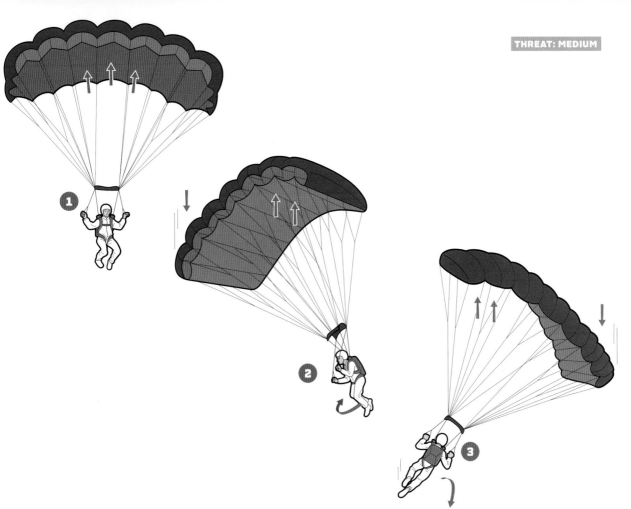

⬆ LAND STRAIGHT.

You have successfully negotiated free fall, deployed your canopy, and are about to touch down. Safe? Nope. Inexperienced solo jumpers trying to avoid an obstacle at the last minute, or experienced skydivers looking for a thrill, might sometimes pull a toggle and enter a low-hook turn. "If you make that turn too low, your parachute doesn't have time to level out," says Nancy Koreen of the United States Parachute Association. Instead, with your weight far out from the canopy, you'll swing down like a wrecking ball.

STAT: In the U.S. in 2012, low-hook turns caused five of 19 skydiving fatalities.

DO: Scope out your landing spot well in advance (from 100 to 1,000 feet up, depending on your skill) so you have room to land without needing to swerve.

Descending on a straight path ❶ becomes perilous when a parachutist attempts a turn too close to the ground ❷ . In midturn, both the canopy and jumper are spiraling down rapidly ❸ . Without enough time and elevation to complete the turn and level out, the jumper hits the ground at a dramatically elevated speed ❹ .

113

Increased awareness of *commotio cordis*—a blow to the chest that causes ventrical fibrillation— has led municipalities and sports leagues to require defibrillators at events including baseball, ice hockey, and lacrosse games.

DODGE LINE DRIVES.

America's national pastime may seem a gentle pursuit, but it is not without its fatal hazards. The 2008 book *Death at the Ballpark: A Comprehensive Study of Game-Related Fatalities, 1862–2007* catalogs deaths that have occurred while people were playing, watching, or officiating at baseball games. Among the causes is *commotio cordis,* a concussion of the heart that leads to ventrical fibrillation when the chest is struck during a critical 10- to 30-millisecond moment between heartbeats. About 50 percent of all victims are athletes (and the vast majority of these are male) engaging in sports that also include ice hockey and lacrosse, the U.S. National Commotio Cordis Registry reports.

STAT: The registry recorded 224 fatal cases from 1996 to 2010. Commotio cordis is the number-one killer in U.S. youth baseball, causing two to three deaths a year.

DON'T: Take a shot to the chest. Even evasive action and protective gear are not significant deterrents.

OF NOTE: Survival rates rose to 35 percent between 2000 and 2010, up from 15 percent in the previous decade, due mainly to the increased presence of defibrillators at sporting events.

KEEP YOUR FOOTING.

One mistake is responsible for about half of all ladder accidents: carrying something while climbing.

STAT: More than 700 people die annually in falls from ladders and scaffolding.

DO: Keep three points of contact while climbing and use work-belt hooks, a rope and pulley, or other means to get items aloft.

STAY WARM AND DRY.

Cold is a deceptive menace—most fatal hypothermia cases occur when it isn't excessively cold, from 30 to 50 degrees Fahrenheit. Wet clothes compound the effect of the temperature.

STAT: Hypothermia kills almost 1,000 people a year in the U.S.

DO: Wear synthetic or wool clothing, not moisture-trapping cotton. If stranded, conserve heat by stuffing your clothes or shelter with dry leaves.

CLIMB WITH CARE.

Accidental shootings are an obvious hazard of hunting, but guess what's just as bad: trees. "A tree stand hung 20 feet in the air should be treated like a loaded gun, because it is every bit as danger-ous," says Marilyn Bentz, executive director of the National Bowhunter Educational Foundation. Most tree-stand accidents occur while a hunter is climbing, she says.

STAT: About 100 hunters a year die falling from trees in the U.S. and Canada, a number "equal to or exceeding firearm-related hunting deaths," Bentz says.

DO: Use a safety harness tethered to the tree when climbing instead of relying on wooden boards nailed to the tree, which can give way suddenly.

AVOID CLIFFING OUT.

Hikers out for a scramble may end up on an uncom-fortably steep patch and, finding it easier to climb up than down, keep ascending until they "cliff out," unable to go either forward or back. Spending a night freezing on a rock face waiting to be rescued is no fun, but the alternative is worse.

STAT: Falls are one of the top three causes of death in the wilderness, along with cardiac arrest and drowning. Cliffed-out hikers account for 11 percent of all search-and-rescue calls in Yosem-ite National Park.

DON'T: Take a shortcut you can't see the length of. If you realize you've lost your way, either back-track or call for help. Gadgets such as DeLorme's inReach SE provide satellite communication to send a distress call from anywhere on the planet.

USE GENERATORS SAFELY.

After Hurricane Sandy, many homeowners used portable generators to replace lost power, leaving the machines running overnight and allowing odorless carbon monoxide to waft inside. The gas induces dizziness, headaches, and nausea in people who are awake, but "when people go to sleep with a generator running, there's no chance for them to realize that something's wrong," says Brett Brenner, president of the Electrical Safety Foundation International.

STAT: Carbon monoxide from consumer prod-ucts, including portable generators, kills nearly 200 a year. Of the Sandy-related deaths, 12 were due to carbon monoxide poisoning.

DO: Keep generators more than 20 feet from a house.

DON'T DRINK TOO MUCH. →

We all know that dehydration can be dangerous, leading to dizziness, seizures, and death, but drink-ing too much water can be just as bad. In 2002, 28-year-old runner Cynthia Lucero collapsed midway through the Boston Marathon. Rushed to a hospital, she fell into a coma and died. In the aftermath it emerged that she had drunk large amounts along the run. The excess liquid in her system induced a syndrome called exercise-associ-ated hyponatremia (EAH), in which an imbalance in the body's sodium levels creates a dangerous swelling of the brain.

STAT: Up to one-third of endurance athletes who collapse during events suffer from EAH. Between 1989 and 1996, when the U.S. Army mandated heavy fluid intake during exercise in high heat, EAH caused at least six deaths.

DON'T: Drink more than one and a half quarts per hour during sustained, intense exercise. But do consume plenty of salt along with your fluids.

Caused by excessive fluid
intake, hyponatremia
can make the brain swell
like a dehydrated sponge
soaked in water.

DON'T SLIP-SLIDE AWAY.

Hikers on a glacier or in areas where patches of snow remain above the tree line may be tempted to speed downhill by sliding, or *glissading*. Bad idea: A gentle glide can easily lead to an unstoppable plummet. In 2005 climber Patrick Wang, 27, died on California's Mount Whitney while glissading off the summit; he slid 300 feet before falling off a 1,000-foot cliff.

STAT: One or two people die each year while glissading.

DON'T: Glissade, period. But if you ever do it, you should be an expert mountaineer with well-practiced self-arrest techniques. Glissaders should always remove their crampons and know their line of descent.

BEAT THE HEAT.

A rock formation in Utah called The Wave is remote and beautiful but also arid and sweltering. In July 2012, a couple hiking the area were found dead after the afternoon heat overwhelmed them. Scarcely three weeks later, a 27-year-old woman collapsed while hiking The Wave with her husband and died before he could get help.

STAT: An average of 675 people die each year in the U.S. from heat-related complications.

DO: Carry lots of fluids, hike in the morning, and let people know where you're going when trekking in the desert.

LET LEANING TREES STAND. ⬇

The motorized blade isn't always the most dangerous thing about using a chainsaw. Trees contain enormous amounts of energy that can release in ways both surprising and lethal. If a tree stands at an angle, it becomes top-heavy and transfers energy lower in the trunk. When sawed, it can shatter midcut and create a so-called barber chair. The fibers split vertically and the rearward half pivots backward. "It's very violent and it's very quick," says Mark Chisholm, chief executive of New Jersey Arborists.

STAT: In 2012, 32 people died felling trees.

DON'T: Saw into any tree or limb that's under tension.

STRATEGY:
HOW TO NAVIGATE WITH A MAP AND COMPASS

Though GPS may seem ubiquitous, it doesn't work everywhere. Mountains and dense tree cover can knock out satellite signals—and batteries can die. Here's how to roam the backcountry with a compass and topo map.

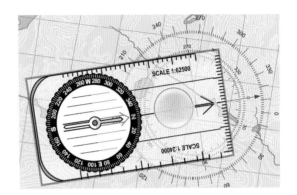

1. Orient the map by aligning its magnetic north (MN) indicator with your compass's reading of MN.

2. Pencil the MN line across the map, then anchor the map in this north-facing position; instead of turning the map as you head toward your destination, pivot around it as if switching seats at a table.

3. Draw a line between where you are and where you want to go. Once you turn toward the destination, the line of travel should be perpendicular to your chest.

4. Fold the map parallel to your line of travel, leaving a two-inch margin on the side that you hold. Place the map between thumb and index finger and begin "thumbing the map"—use your thumb to check off terrain features as you travel so you can look away from the map without losing your bearings.

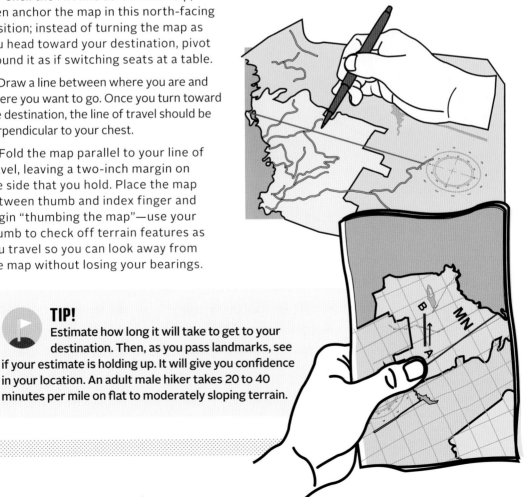

TIP!
Estimate how long it will take to get to your destination. Then, as you pass landmarks, see if your estimate is holding up. It will give you confidence in your location. An adult male hiker takes 20 to 40 minutes per mile on flat to moderately sloping terrain.

Keep your guard up.
If your hands have
to come all the way
up from your sides,
you will telegraph
your strike.

How to Throw a Punch

STAND WITH YOUR nondominant foot forward, with 30 percent of your weight on your front foot and 70 percent on your back. Make sure your fist is tight with your thumb outside your fingers. Pivot on the ball of your rear foot and twist your waist in toward your target, carrying the energy up your back and down your arm. Drive your dominant arm forward and connect with the knuckles of your pointer finger, middle finger, and ring finger. For maximum effectiveness, imagine you are punching through your opponent. Walls are ill-advised opponents.

GETTING STARTED IN:

Snowshoeing

THE BEST WAY TO EXERCISE AND EXPLORE ALL WINTER.

WHY SNOWSHOE?

Unless you're a skier, the snow-covered terrain of winter can mean four months inside wondering what the sun used to look like. But not if you have a pair of snowshoes. They make the outside world accessible year-round while requiring no more skill than what it takes to walk to the couch. We asked Mark Elmore, sports director of the United States Snowshoe Association, to walk us through the basics. After that, we headed outside.

THE VARIETIES

The snowshoes you use depend on the terrain you plan on covering and how long you'll be out. But in general, remember: The deeper the snow and the heavier your load, the larger the shoe you'll need to stay on top of the snow.

RECREATIONAL

What most snowshoers end up using. The standard size is eight by 25 inches. If you're heavier than average, find a shoe that's a bit longer. If you're lighter than average, choose something smaller, like eight by 22 inches. Be sure to look at the size and types of boots a snowshoe's bindings will accommodate. Some can even fit snowboard boots, if you happen to already own them. Most important on the bindings, Elmore says, is to have a secure connection and a wide range of motion that lets you walk normally.

BACKCOUNTRY

Larger snowshoes that allow you to travel in deep powder and support the weight of multiday hiking packs. Standard sizes range from nine by 30 inches to 10 by 36 inches, depending on your weight and the weight of the gear you typically carry.

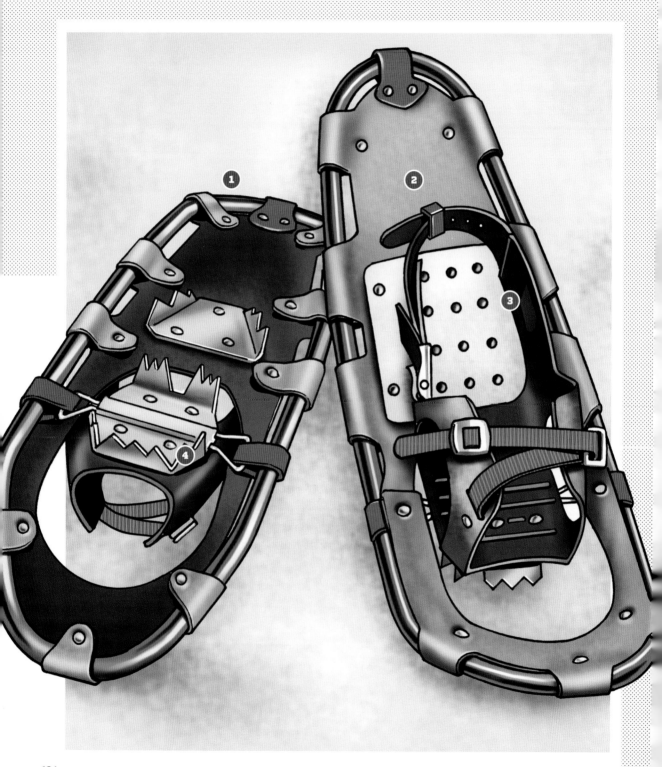

SNOWSHOES

Snowshoes come in a variety of materials. The originals, which many people still use today, were wood and rawhide. They are beautiful but can slip on hard-packed snow. Plastic snowshoes are lightweight and inexpensive but lack durability. There are carbon-fiber options, too, but those are expensive enough that they're used only by true aficionados. In the U.S. most people choose aluminum. It's relatively light and durable and doesn't require you to pawn family heirlooms to purchase.

THE PARTS

1 Framing: Gives the snowshoe its structure. Width on most pairs is relatively similar, but length changes drastically depending on the type of snow that's typical in your area. (The deeper and dryer the powder, the longer the shoe.)

2 Decking: Provides surface area to disperse weight and support you on top of the snow. Typically made of nylon.

3 Binding: Adjustable straps, buckles, or ratchets that keep your foot firmly attached to the snowshoe

4 Crampons: Metal plates with teeth to grip into the snow and ice for traction

> **TIP!**
> If you already own hiking poles, save yourself some money and just buy snow baskets. They give the tips of the poles more surface area—and another season of use.

OTHER GEAR

According to Elmore, it is not the snowshoe or even the location that determines the quality of your snowshoe experience. It's how you dress. As with any outdoor winter activity, make sure you wear layers to allow you to regulate your body temperature. And remember to bring food and water. A few other snowshoe-specific pieces of gear to consider:

BOOTIES

You're not going to be warm and comfortable if your feet aren't warm and comfortable, so start with waterproof hiking or winter boots and always wear thick wool socks. Elmore recommends neoprene snowshoe booties as an easy way to add warmth and weather protection to whatever footwear you choose. Try: **Crescent Moon booties**

POLES

Help you balance on the snow and distribute some of the work to your arms and upper back. Poles are especially helpful through deep snow and on uphill and downhill trails. Try: **Redfeather 3-Section Fast Lock poles**

WHERE TO GO

IF THERE IS SNOW, YOU CAN SNOWSHOE. YOU JUST MIGHT FEEL A LITTLE SILLY IF IT'S LESS THAN SIX INCHES.

Where you are: A state park in New England
What to expect: Unless the region is in the midst of a particular cold snap, you'll usually encounter dense snow with a higher moisture content according to Elmore. "It packs much easier so you don't need as much surface area on your decking," he says. Snow of this variety is great for beginners. Less chance of tripping over yourself.

Where you are: The Colorado backcountry
What to expect: Three feet of powdery snow covering uneven terrain. In deep, drier snow, "You're going to want bigger shoes so that you're staying on top of the snow and not sinking into it, making your work harder," Elmore says. While it will be fun, it will also be tough. Snowshoe poles will help you keep your balance as the snow shifts and moves beneath you.

Where you are: Anywhere with a groomed trail
What to expect: Hard-packed snow that might be icy. Many skiing areas and local parks offer groomed snowshoe trails. Here's where you can try moving much more quickly on smaller shoes. When you get really confident, you can enter a race. (For options check snowshoeracing.com.)

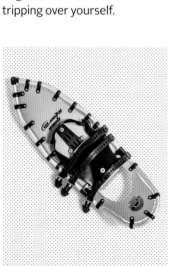

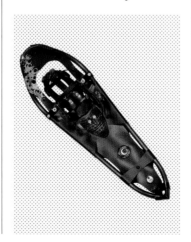

How to Make a Whiskey Torch

When you've polished off a nicely shaped bottle of whiskey (or your preferred drink), wash it and peel off the label. Fill it halfway with tiki-torch fuel. Feed a fiberglass tiki wick through a small copper coupling ($\frac{1}{2}$ to $\frac{5}{8}$ inch). Fit this into a larger coupling ($\frac{5}{8}$ to $\frac{3}{4}$ inch). Place this in the mouth of the bottle. Set it on your patio table, light the wick, and open another bottle.

How to Lock Valuables Down with Chains

I'VE GOT A VACATION CABIN AND FOR THE FIRST TIME WE'VE HAD REPEATED BREAK-INS AND SOME THEFT. TO INCREASE SECURITY, I WAS THINKING OF CHAINING A FEW VALUABLES DOWN. IS THERE A CHAIN THAT CAN'T BE CUT WITH BOLT CUTTERS?

THE SHORT ANSWER is yes, you can get cut-resistant chain. It's hardened throughout its thickness, and its flat face distributes the force of the bolt cutter's jaw over a wide area, thereby diffusing it. There are also industrial high-strength welded steel chains that are through-hardened. The larger diameters of these chains, especially the ⅝-, ¾-, and ⅞-inch sizes, are extremely difficult to cut due to their girth and hardness. (Note we said difficult, not impossible; there are industrial bolt cutters that have jaw sizes as large as ¾ inch and are designed to cut hardened steel.) Industrial chain is rated by grades; the higher the grade number, the more steel alloying elements it contains and the more resistant it is to the variety of loads a chain encounters, especially in tension. Grades 70, 80, and 100 are among the hardest and toughest available. Here's the kicker, though. We're talking chain that costs $10 to $22 per foot; it's likely to be more valuable than what you're chaining down, a fact that might not be lost on an enterprising thief, who might just make off with the chain itself!

Regardless of how strong the chain is, you'd also need a cut-resistant padlock, such as a shrouded model by Master Lock or Sobo. You might also have to attach the chain to something secure, such as a concrete footing. Likewise, hasps, bars, and bolts have to be thick and impregnable. It doesn't take much to deter a lazy thief, but it takes a lot to keep out one who's determined to get in, if for no other reason than to prove his point. Any weak link (if you'll excuse the pun) invites trouble in the form of a bolt cutter, an oversize crowbar, or—don't laugh—a chain hooked to a large pickup truck. We heard a story about one guy whose home was burglarized by a thief who used the rear bumper of his pickup truck as a battering ram, which he put through the front door.

We might be stating the obvious here, but cabin

> **It doesn't take much to deter a lazy thief, but it takes a lot to keep out a determined one.**

When your property is left unattended for long periods of time, thieves notice.

owners have relied on some pretty low-tech security measures over the years. First, make friends with local families and fellow cabin owners. In all but a few communities, people look out for one another. Next, don't store anything in the cabin or an outbuilding that you'd be afraid to lose. Keep power tools, chainsaws, outboard motors, or other gear elsewhere. There may be a local business that can store equipment for you for a fee or a nearby storage facility. Sure, stopping on the way to the cabin is a nuisance, but so is having your property stolen.

Finally, alert the local authorities when you're away. Some rural police departments have added four-wheel-drive vehicles, snow sleds, and ATVs to their fleet, making it possible for them to patrol remote areas.

3 Ways to Roast a Whole Pig

CHEF SEAN BROCK HAS ROASTED HUNDREDS OF PIGS FOR HIS RESTAURANTS. IF YOU'RE STUCK WITHOUT A TRADITIONAL KITCHEN—BUT YOU DO HAVE A PIG—YOU CAN USE HIS METHODS TO COOK IT.

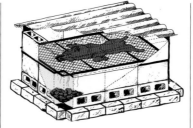

1. Spit. "You keep turning it to get an even, golden-brown crust," Brock says. "It's a bit faster, but it's open-air, so you lose some of the smoky flavor." Pick a stainless steel one.

2. Concrete-block pit. "I prefer this method," he says. "It gives you the control to cook the pig slowly, moving the coals around until it's tender." See globetrotterdiaries.com/recipes/a-beginners-guide-to-roasting-a-whole-pig.

3. La Caja China roaster. "You put the pig in the box with charcoal on top," Brock says. "It makes for moist meat, and it's almost foolproof, but it doesn't give the wood flavor that I'm obsessed with." From lacajachina.com.

STRATEGY:
HOW TO BUTCHER A PIG

Back Fat

Loin

Shoulder

Spare Ribs

Leg / Ham

Side / Belly

Jowl

Hock

Trotters

YOU CAN DO most of the work with a five- to six-inch semi-flexible boning knife. To work on bones, you'll need a saw with bigger teeth or a cleaver. Remove the head, trotters, hocks, and tenderloin, then separate the pig into "primals." This means separating the back leg (the ham) and the front leg (the shoulder) from the middle section and splitting the middle section into loin (chops) and belly (bacon). Next, turn the primals into subprimals. On the shoulder, for instance, this means separating the picnic roast from the Boston butt. From there, trim, sculpt, and debone the meat into the cuts you see at the meat counter. Remember: If you screw up, you can always make sausage.

GETTING STARTED IN:

Curing Meat

THE MOST COUNTERINTUITIVE WAY OF PREPARING MEAT CAN ALSO BE THE MOST DELICIOUS.

CURING YOUR OWN MEAT involves seasoning, table salt, curing salt, and a whole lot of patience. The time between buying a cut of meat from the butcher to actually serving it at the table can be months. Or even years. That's when the meat breaks down, unlocking flavor you could never cook into it. If you're concerned about the wisdom of holding on to a slab of pork for two months before eating it, that's good. You should be. But science will keep you safe. The salt and cure mix draw moisture out of the meat, and without moisture, bacteria and pathogens cannot germinate and the meat doesn't spoil. You just have to do it right.

GATHER YOUR SUPPLIES

MEAT
If you have a recipe, it will tell you what cut of meat to use. Most of the time that cut will be pork shoulder, also called pork butt or Boston butt. Relatively inexpensive and with around a 30 percent fat composition, pork butt is perfect for sausage. For meats that require a different proportion of fat, you can also buy a leaner cut and a separate slab of fatback, then grind them together.

CURING SALT
A mixture of table salt and sodium nitrite. It adds flavor and color and prevents meat from going bad. There are two options: Insta Cure No. 1 or Insta Cure No. 2. (See below.)

SAUSAGE GRINDER
Any meat that's going to become sausage has to be ground before it'll go in casing. For most hobbyists, a hand-cranked grinder will work just fine. The LEM Products No. 10 clamps to your counter and costs under $100. Or if you already have a stand mixer you can buy a grinder attachment for even less.

CASINGS
Sections of the inner lining of animal intestines hold sausages together. (Synthetic options are more durable, but they have a substantial effect on taste. Skip them.) Pick based on the size of your final product. The standard is 32- to 35-mm hog casings. You'll also find 19- to 21-mm sheep casings and 40- to 43-mm cow casings, which tend to be too big and complicated for beginners.

SAUSAGE STUFFER
A large container with a plunger operated by hand crank. Turn the crank to extrude the meat into the casing. Some grinders come with a sausage-stuffing attachment but a stand-alone stuffer will be more efficient and hygienic.

SAUSAGE PRICKER
Use these sharp tines to puncture any air bubbles you see in your links.

HOW IT WORKS:
Insta Cure

Nitrite (NO_2) draws the water out of meat, preventing bacteria such as *Clostridium botulinum* (which causes botulism) and other pathogens from germinating. **Insta Cure No. 1** is a mixture of salt and sodium nitrite ($NaNO_2$) and should be used for short-duration cures that sit for a couple of days to a couple of weeks, like capicola or mortadella. After that the nitrite becomes inert and the curing process halts. For longer-curing meats such as chorizo or prosciutto, **Insta Cure No. 2** adds sodium nitrate ($NaNO_3$). After the initial nitrite stops working, the nitrate molecules (NO_3) give up oxygen atoms and turn into additional nitrite to finish the job.

MAKE SOME SAUSAGE

1. Cut meat and fat into 1½-inch chunks and feed into the grinder with a handful of crushed ice. Add the spice mix from your recipe and mix thoroughly. You're ready to stuff.

2. Rinse the brine off the casings and soak them in warm water for at least an hour. Wet the table and the horn of the stuffer to deter tearing.

3. Tie off the casing and thread it onto the horn until only a few inches are free. If there are air pockets, lightly prick the tube with your sausage pricker.

4. Put your mixture in the stuffer's hopper. Work the hopper with one hand while using the other to control the rate at which meat fills the casing.

5. When all your meat is packed, cut and tie off the casing.

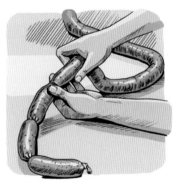

6. One hand's length from the end, pinch and twist a few times to form a link. Repeat, twisting in the opposite direction. Continue until the entire sausage is in links.

TIP!
Don't freeze natural casings—it ruins their integrity. Keep them in their brine, or, if you've rinsed some and then realized you don't need them all, cover them in salt and refrigerate in a sealed container, where they will last for a full year.

135

CURE THE MEAT

There are three common methods for curing any meat: drying, fermenting, and smoking.

SMOKING

The easiest of the curing methods, smoking can be done on a standard kettle grill. Here's how:

• Presoak your wood chips in water for an hour.
• Set charcoal on one side of the grill. When the flame has burned off, add the wood chips.
• Put the meat on the side without coals, close the lid, and open the vents above the meat side of the grill.
• Smoke the meat to an internal temperature of 110°F, then put it in an oven set to 300°F, slowly bringing the internal temperature of the meat to 155°F.

DRYING

Dry boxes provide a temperature- and humidity-controlled environment for your meat. You can buy one for around $1,500 or you make your own out of an empty refrigerator, an automatic thermostat, a fan, a humidifier, and a dehumidifier. The dry box keeps the meat at 58°F and 83 percent humidity. Your recipe will tell you how long to dry the meat, but as a general rule, meat is ready to eat when it weighs less than half of its initial raw weight.

FERMENTING

Tangy sausages like salami are made by adding acid-producing bacteria (available at meat hobbyist sites such as butcher-packer.com). The meat ferments in a climate-controlled chamber—like that dry box you just built, but set to 73°F and a humidity level of 95 percent. You'll need MicroFine pH paper (also available at butcher-packer.com) to periodically test the pH of the meat and determine if enough lactic acid is present to make it safe.

SAFETY

Without proper sanitization, preparation, and storage, illnesses like botulism can flourish—at which point the number of people interested in your home-cured salami diminishes greatly. A few tips:

• Keep raw meat below 44°F unless you're about to cook it or start fermenting.
• Put all equipment in the freezer half an hour before you start. When grinding, process a small amount of meat at a time and grind into a bowl nestled in a larger bowl filled with ice.
• Sterilize your workstation, equipment, hands, and anything else that may come in contact with meat.
• Use the right amount of *cure mix*—table salt and curing salt. The amount is based on a percentage of the weight of the meat you're using:
Steamed sausage (e.g., bratwurst): 1.5 percent table salt, no curing salt
Cooked meat that is consumed cold (e.g., ham): 2.7 percent table salt, 0.2 percent curing salt
Dry cured meat: 2.5 to 4 percent table salt (depending on size), 0.5 percent curing salt
Salami: 2.6 percent table salt, 0.2 percent curing salt
• During the first stage, keep your meat refrigerated at 33 to 35 degrees.

Techniques requiring more time and precision to get right are riskier to get wrong.

Low Risk — Smoking — Fresh sausage — Dry-curing — Fermenting — High Risk

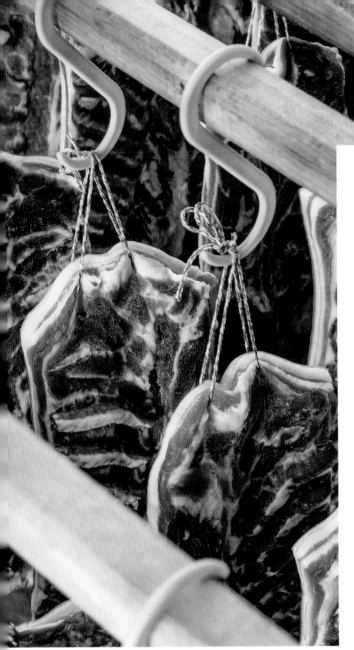

THE STARTER RECIPE:
Flat Pancetta

This recipe, from the Olympia Provisions cookbook, gives you the option of cooking the meat like bacon after curing or, if you have a dry box, letting it dry, slicing it thin, and really impressing your friends.

INGREDIENTS

1 tbsp	crushed black pepper
1½ tbsp	crushed juniper berries
¼ tsp	freshly grated nutmeg
2 tsp	chopped garlic
2	bay leaves
5 sprigs	thyme
3 tbsp	fine sea salt
1¾ tbsp	brown sugar
1¾ tsp	Insta Cure No. 2
4 lb	pork belly, skin-on

1. Combine spices, salt, sugar, and Insta Cure No. 2 (page 132). Sprinkle a generous coating of this mix on the bottom of an airtight container. Lay the pork belly on top, then cover with the rest of the mix. Seal the container and refrigerate for one week.
2. Take the container out of the fridge, flip over the pork belly, then reseal and refrigerate for an additional week.
3. Open the container, remove the meat, and swish around the liquids and salt. Put the meat back in, then everything goes in the fridge, uncovered, for four more days.
4. You're done—if you want to be. You can cook it now: Rinse the meat off, slice it thin, and fry it up. Perfect as a pizza topping. Or continue to step 5.
5. Thoroughly rinse the pancetta, then hang it in a dry box for 35 days. Then slice it up and serve.

TIP!
If you see unwanted mold on your salami, wipe it away with vinegar. Its high acidity lowers the pH level, killing the mold. Vinegar is also a great natural way to keep your dry box sanitized during the curing process. Wipe down the walls of your dry box with a vinegar-soaked cloth twice per week.

How to Make a Rocket Stove

A USEFUL CAMPFIRE ALTERNATIVE

ROCKET STOVES ARE HIGHLY EFFICIENT, thanks to a strong draft. Instead of needing full-size logs, which may not be readily available in an emergency, rocket stoves can use sticks and leaves to produce a flame hot enough to boil water or cook breakfast. Just add a trivet or a burner grate as a cooking surface, and you'll be eating in no time.

1. On flat ground, lay one block with the holes facing out. This will support the burn chamber above it.

2. Stand another block vertically against the end of that first block. You will feed your leaves and sticks in the top hole of this block.

3. Form an H-shape with the brick and pavers on top of the first block. Make sure your brick, when standing on the end, is the same height as the pavers standing on their sides. (Standard bricks are approximately eight inches high.) The brick sandwiched between the pavers should provide the same width as the concrete block below it.

4. Stack the final block on top of the H shape, making sure that the chambers align.

5. Build your fire in the top hole nearest the vertical block. Once your fire is burning steadily, you're ready to cook.

Saviors of the Snowed-In

EVERYTHING YOU NEED TO GET THAT BLIZZARD OFF YOUR DRIVEWAY.

1.
ALUMINUM COMBO SHOVEL

This type of shovel has a hybrid head that can push snow or lift it and a handle that allows you to stand, not stoop. No stooping.

4.
SNOW BRUSH

The design of a good snow brush allows you to reach into awkward nooks on your car where snow can hide, like beneath the wipers or behind the spare tire. And if it has a foam head, you can be aggressive without accidentally scratching the paint.

2.
ICE MELTER

A good deicer not only melts the ice you've got now, it also prevents the next storm from forming more of it. Best if you can accomplish both tasks without poisoning your concrete, your pets, or the environment.

5.
NONSTICK SPRAY

Coating your shovel with a slippery polymer before shoveling prevents snow from sticking to it and slowing you down. It's like spraying a frying pan with PAM but, you know, for tools.

3.
GLOVES

Waterproof. Kevlar-reinforced. Insulated. All good things to look for. And unlike the ski gloves you might have planned to use, the right gloves allow you to move your fingers.

6.
THERMOS

When you're ready to take a break—and you will be—you want an insulated bottle, ideally one that can be opened with one hand, even in gloves. Pro tip: A splash of Irish whiskey vastly improves both coffee and cocoa.

ADVICE FROM A LIFELONG SHOVELER: As much as I love machines, I don't need another one to look after. So I don't use a snowblower. I shovel, and I have for more than 40 years, since I was a kid in Connecticut. The difference between now and then is that these days I'm smarter. I've learned that it's better to push the snow than lift it. If I do have to pick up snow, I hold the shovel close to my body. It's simple physics: The farther out you extend a full shovel, the harder you have to work. My method: I clear a strip along the edge of the driveway and then push all the snow into it. Then I go work on something else. No sense spending all day pushing around old weather.
—*Roy Berendsohn*

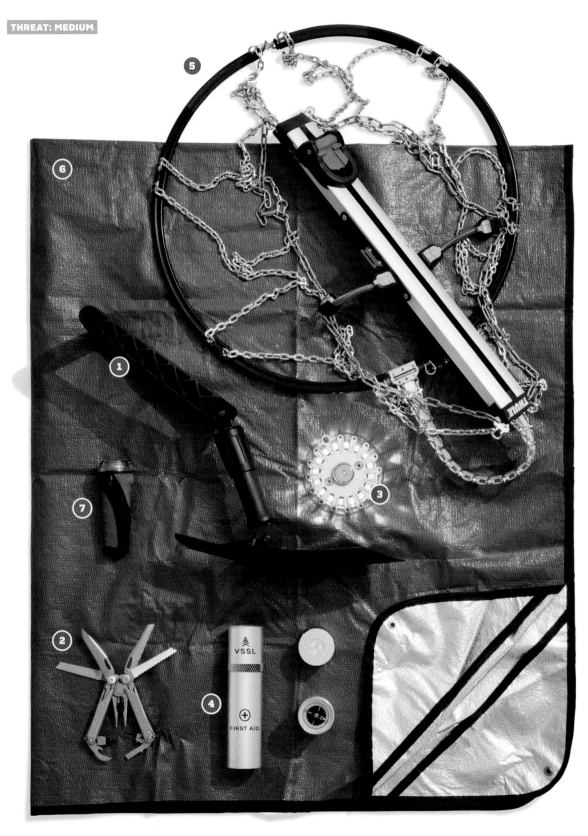

The Ultimate All-Weather Road Kit

WHEN DRIVING IN SNOW, ICE, HEAVY RAIN, OR EXTREME COLD, YOUR ODDS OF MAKING IT HOME COULD DEPEND ON WHAT YOU'VE GOT IN THE TRUNK.

1.
FOLDING SPADE

A regular shovel is too large to carry around all the time, so get a foldable one thatcan chop through the nastiest of frozen snow and muck. The good ones also have sharp picks in the event that tree roots, rocks, or zombie snow wolves are what stand between you and the open road.

4.
FIRST-AID KIT

You probably keep a first-aid kit in your car already, but consider changing it out for a more versatile option. The best have the usual bandages, antiseptics, and tweezers, along with rubber gloves, a backup flashlight, and a roll of medical tape you could use for repairs in a pinch.

2.
MULTITOOL

Tim O'Neil, owner and president of Team O'Neil Rally School, puts it this way: "Everyone has a Leatherman, so sometimes I'll try to use a multitool from another company just to see what I think. Then the screwdriver bit will break off. That's why everyone has a Leatherman."

5.
TIRE CHAINS

The worst time to apply chains is right when you realize you need them. Get easy-on versions and save your frozen hands. Most snap over tires in 15 seconds apiece.

3.
SAFETY LIGHTS

If you got yourself into this mess, other drivers will get themselves into this mess as well. Keep yourself well-lit and out of their way.

6.
SPACE BLANKET

It's useful in the event of heat loss and you can also stick it under your tires to gain traction when you're spinning your wheels in a snowbank.

7.
SPOTLIGHT

Consider the conditions in which you'll be using your flashlight: You want one that's waterproof, long-lasting, and bright as heck. Some options even have an SOS mode.

How to Handle Driving Trouble

IF YOU'RE HYDROPLANING

Ease off the throttle and keep the tires pointed where you want to go. It seems simple, but when the wheel stops responding, our natural reaction is to turn it further. Then, when the tires get traction again, the car gets jerked in that direction, which you don't want.

IF YOU'RE STUCK IN MUD

Let the wheels spin with the engine at 3,000 to 4,000 rpm to give your tires the best chance of digging in. Then "saw" the steering wheel: Quickly turn it back and forth about 90 degrees to the left and 90 degrees to the right. This allows the front tires to find purchase.

IF YOU CAN'T SEE THROUGH YOUR WINDSHIELD

The only good wiper blades are new wiper blades. Even expensive ones go bad. So just put new, cheap ones on more often. Twice a year is good. If you don't have new blades on you, you can use really fine, wet sandpaper, like 400-grit, to remove the nicks in your old ones.

IF YOU REALLY, REALLY NEED TO STOP

Trust your antilock braking system. Hold the brake pedal down as far as it will go. Remember, though, if you have to steer to avoid something, you'll have to come off the brakes a bit. If 100 percent of a tire's grip is being used for braking, it cannot also steer.

If your skin feels numb and turns white or gray-yellow, you may already have frostbite.

Five Medical Myths

BURN

MYTH:
Put butter on it
SKILL:
Sorry, grandma. Cold running water is the immediate emollient of choice for minor first-degree burns. Once the burn has cooled, try ibuprofen and topical creams or sprays. For small second-degree burns (blisters; white, dead skin) get soap and water, antiseptic cream, and a bandage. For larger or more severe burns, get to a doctor or the ER.

FROSTBITE

MYTH:
Rub snow on the affected area
SKILL:
No. At the first sign of tingling, pain, or numbness in the fingers, toes, ears, or nose, get inside and get warm. Dunk the frostbitten parts in warm water—the temperature of a hot tub—for 10 minutes. (The process can be painful; take some ibuprofen.) As the water cools, keep warming it back up to 100° to 105° F. If hot water is unavailable, lightly compress the frosted parts against your—or somebody else's—armpit or groin. Do not rub the affected area.

SNAKEBITE

MYTH:
Cut open the wound and suck out the venom.
SKILL:
Save your lips. The fastest, simplest treatment is antivenin. Unless you are sure the snake was not venomous, call 911 or get yourself to the ER immediately. Minimize physical activity and lightly wrap the arm or leg just above the bite to limit swelling and slow the spread of venom. Antivenin is widely available and easy to administer. According to Dr. Mark Ryan of the Louisiana Poison Center, "the chances of dying from a snakebite in the U.S. are quite small."

SEIZURES

MYTH:
Shove a spoon in the victim's mouth so he won't swallow his tongue.
SKILL:
It's physically impossible to swallow your tongue. In fact, there's little you can do to help a seizure victim except to roll him on his side into the "recovery position," remove hard or sharp items from the area, and seek medical attention. Don't try to restrain him; it can only cause injury.

TICKS

MYTH:
Burn it off with a cigarette
SKILL:
The goal is not to inflict pain on the little sucker (and probably yourself), but to remove the entire tick, including its embedded mouth parts. Using dull tweezers (sharp ones may cut off the body, leaving the head), pull the tick gently and steadily away from the skin. It may take a minute or two to gradually extract it, so be patient.

4.

Threat: High

CATASTROPHE STRUCK, BUT YOUR
FAMILY IS SAFE. YOU NEED TO MOVE
AND QUICKLY.

CHECKLIST:

The Other Survival Checklist

GALLON JUGS OF WATER, FIRE EXTINGUISHERS, AND FIRST-AID SUPPLIES ARE THE ESSENTIALS OF ANY GOOD SURVIVAL KIT (LIKE THE IDEAL SURVIVAL KIT, PAGE 54), BUT OUR SURVEY OF THOSE WHO OUTLASTED DISASTERS SUGGESTS A FEW MORE UNEXPECTED ITEMS.

BEER

"Buy a lot of it," says Trey Click, a magazine publisher who rode out 2008's Hurricane Ike in Galveston, Texas. "It's one of the only things you can use for money in the aftermath." Need your neighbor to help you clear trees out of your yard? A case of Bud is a better motivator than a $20 bill when all the stores are boarded up.

HANDHELD CB RADIO

Think no one uses CB radios anymore? Think again. These things can be a direct line to emergency crews and tow trucks—exactly the folks you might want to get in touch

with after a disaster. Plus they work when cell towers don't. Look for one that also tunes into NOAA weather channels.

CONTRACTOR BAGS

Thick, sturdy three-mil contractor bags are the multitool of the disaster world. They're tough enough to stuff with sharp debris, they work as an impromptu poncho or water barrier for leaky structures, and you can use them to drag heavy objects.

GLOW BRACELETS

When the electricity is out, you may not feel like celebrating, but these party

favors can come in handy. "Houses get dark really quickly with no power," says Mark Vorderbruggen, who went five days without electricity after Ike hit Texas. "I used them to mark the location of radios, flashlights, batteries, and door handles."

A GOOD BOOK

When stuck in his Jeep for two weeks, Daryl Jané would have killed for a good book. "I had water and a sleeping bag, and that's all you really need to survive," he says. "But it gets so boring after a while. If I'd had a book I would have been set."

Consider the Ham Radio

FOR EMERGENCIES OR JUST IDLE CHATTER.

BY JASON FEIFER

"THIS IS KD4DYV," I said, announcing my ham-radio call sign for the first time in 20 years. "Can anyone hear me?"

I fiddled with my old handheld radio, an Icom IC-W2A, and tried again. Nothing. The radio was all that remained of a childhood hobby, back when I also had a 32-foot antenna in my parents' backyard and a Morse-code key for tapping out messages. The technical name for all this is amateur radio, an old-timey pursuit in which operators pass a test, get a license and call sign from the Federal Communications Commission, then spend their days chitchatting across the globe. The term ham was once an insult, a name pros gave to amateurs with clumsy Morse skills and mediocre equipment.

When I joined as a squeaky-voiced 12-year-old in the 1990s, it was like discovering the internet before the internet. Ham is built upon the thrill of the contact: Operators routinely hold contests to reach, say, someone in every state, or they clamor to talk with a fuzzy voice floating in from some far-off island. But then I grew up. Last fall my dad found my expired ham license. At first I filed it away as a memento. But then I remembered: When a disaster strikes, ham radios are pivotal to survival. Operators become community lifelines, talking to each other and working with first responders. I still owned my old handheld and it seemed foolish not to have it at the ready. So I renewed my license and set about seeing how ham has fared in the digital age.

The answer: quite well. There are now almost 725,000 licensed hams in the U.S., an increase of almost 200,000 since I bailed two decades ago. In part this is because of new technology that enables talk on previously inaccessible frequencies. And to encourage newcomers, the FCC no longer requires that hams know Morse code. There's also a new smartphone app called EchoLink that patches hams into *transmission repeaters,* devices that receive weak signals and retransmit them with more juice.

With my radio busted, I downloaded EchoLink and found a repeater near my neighborhood. "This is KD4DYV," I said again. "Can anyone hear me?" This time a voice rose from the static: It was Zane, a dad who lives down the street and who earned his license two months ago. Zane recommended buying a $30 Baofeng UV-5R. "I'm on this repeater pretty often," he said, inviting me to return. I will, with my new radio. It's good to know I can reach a friendly voice. Hopefully just to chat but also just in case.

Lodgepole, Nebraska, June 2012

Tornadoes: The Scientific Companion

A COMPREHENSIVE GUIDE TO UNDERSTANDING AND
SURVIVING ONE OF NATURE'S LEAST PREDICTABLE—AND
MOST DANGEROUS—PHENOMENA.

Gurley, Nebraska,
June 22, 2012

 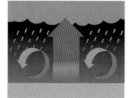  

HOW THEY START

THE FORMATION

1. Warm, moist air, usually from the south, is lifted by a warm or cold front, causing an updraft. The moisture condenses into clouds and precipitation and forms a thunderstorm.
2. Precipitation should counter the updraft, but when winds blow precipitation out of the rising air, the updraft strengthens. Beneath the storm, winds of different speeds (shear) form horizontal tubes of rotating air.
3. When those tubes are ingested into the updraft, they become vertical and the storm acquires rotation, forming a supercell.
4. The rotating tube is stretched and the supercell becomes like a giant vacuum, sucking air up and away. As air rushes in to equalize the pressure, a tornado is formed.

DISASTER PHYSICS

How a Tornado Throws a Car

It's the same principle that gets a 747 off the ground: Intense winds flowing over the top of a car create aerodynamic lift, in which there is less air pressure above than in and under the car. Once the car lifts, the winds get underneath it and raise it higher or just slam it around. The strength of the forces applied to the car grows with the cube of the wind speed. So if the wind doubles in speed, it exerts eight times as much force on the car.

THE RATINGS

Tornadoes are categorized by wind speed, typically determined after the fact through damage assessments. The Enhanced Fujita Scale, or EF, is named for Dr. Theodore Fujita, a storm researcher at the University of Chicago.

EF0 .... **3-sec gusts of 65 to 85 mph.** 63 percent of tornadoes are EF0 or EF1.

EF1 .... **3-sec gusts of 86 to 110 mph.** Can push a shed off its foundation. EF0 and EF1 storms cause less than 5 percent of all tornado deaths.

EF2 .... **3-sec gusts of 111 to 135 mph.** Can destroy building walls and roofs.

EF3 .... **3-sec gusts of 136 to 165 mph.** Marked by thicker funnels. Along with EF2, accounts for 35 percent of tornadoes and 30 percent of deaths.

EF4 .... **3-sec gusts of 166 to 200 mph.** Only 2 percent of tornadoes reach EF4 or EF5.

EF5 .... **3-sec gusts of over 200 mph.** With EF4, accounts for 65 percent of deaths. Winds can twist 20-story buildings.

TORNADO COUNTRY

Tornadoes can form anywhere, at any time of year, but most occur between April and July, either in the Southeast or a swath of the Midwest that rises from Texas to South Dakota.

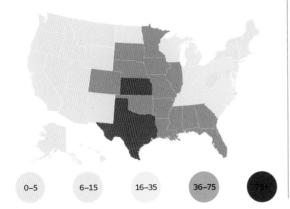

0–5   6–15   16–35   36–75   75+

THE CHASERS

Emily Sutton, Oklahoma City

What's so incredible about tornadoes is that they're beautiful and destructive and mysterious. It's surreal. You feel panicked, excited, scared, and heartbroken, all at the same time.

I was in the path of the Moore, Oklahoma, tornado on May 20, 2013. We were slamming south on the highway and when we pull off at an exit, we're staring at an EF5 bearing down on the town. It looks fake, almost like a backdrop. Then you see debris floating around it in a way that feels peaceful, like a snow globe. Then all of a sudden your heart sinks because you realize that people are dying. You feel guilty because it's inevitable that people are going to die and there is nothing you can do. There are homes, cars, and people being thrown in front of you at that moment.

We rushed straight south and got out of its path and then I felt debris falling from the sky like rain. It was black in front of me. I'd never seen that before.

We watched the storm eventually rope out but at that point we didn't know what had happened because the phones were out.

When another storm chaser, Tim Samaras, died 10 days later, I was only a mile down the road from him. It really reminds you of the power of nature and how tornadoes need to be respected. Just because we have all of these fancy gadgets, that's not going to protect you.

HOW TO FIGHT THEM

THREE CRAZY WAYS TO PREVENT TORNADOES

Tornadoes release built-up pressure in the atmosphere. If we could eliminate them, the atmosphere would have to find another, possibly even more destructive, form of release. But that hasn't stopped people from trying.

Tornado Walls

THEORY: Walls 1,000 feet high and 150 feet wide would disrupt the air movement that allows tornadoes to form.

PROBLEM: A simulation found that the walls needed to be more than 8,000 feet high to be effective.

Microwaves

THEORY: Removing the cold air of a tornado by heating up the storms with microwave-shooting satellites.

PROBLEM: Supercells generate energy on the scale of nuclear warheads, which would get a little expensive.

Cloud Seeding

THEORY: Seeding a developing storm would cause dissipating precipitation.

PROBLEM: You can't prove that a storm acted the way it did because of seeding, so there is no way to prove its efficacy.

THE NEW TECHNOLOGY
A More Targeted Warning System

Traditionally, whether a tornado shows up one mile away or 30, if it's in your county, a siren goes off. But rarely is an entire county at risk, which means that people become accustomed to hearing the siren without seeing a tornado. After a few false alarms, it's easy to stop taking the sirens seriously. To combat this, in 2007 the National Weather Service began targeting *polygons,* geographic areas as much as 80 percent smaller than entire counties. But many counties didn't have the necessary technology, and county-wide sirens continued. WeatherWarn is a simple solution: a software-based siren controller that automatically activates the correct sirens. It also works with smartphones and social media for areas that are not covered by sirens.

A New Doppler

The Doppler radar system used by the weather service since the 1990s had a limitation: It was one-dimensional. The microwaves it sent out were all oriented horizontally, which meant the system could determine if precipitation was light or heavy but it could not tell you if that precipitation was rain or snow. In 2013 the weather service upgraded all its equipment to dual-polarization Doppler radar, which uses microwaves oriented in both directions. Coupled with enhanced computer processing to handle the additional data, the weather service radar system can now determine the size and shape of exactly what is in the air.

The Power of Sound

Because radar works by bouncing off things, it's hindered when hills, trees, and other non-weather objects get in the way. As an alternative, infrasonic arrays measure super-low-frequency sounds, such as the signature wind action of tornadoes. Those sound waves can travel very far, allowing severe storm activity to be observed from more than 600 miles away.

And Lightning

Research suggests lightning occurs frequently in developing tornadoes, so scientists are using networks of electrical sensors called Lightning Mapping Arrays to measure the radio-frequency impulses generated by lightning. By pinpointing lightning's location, data can be returned in as little as one minute, as opposed to five to 10 for radar.

The Simulator

In 2014 Leigh Orf, a professor of atmospheric science at Central Michigan University, and his team presented the first-ever 3-D simulation of an EF5 tornado. The simulation provides a way to study a storm in great detail and from any perspective, which cannot be done with live storms. The better you can understand a fake storm, the easier it is to predict a real one.

A FEW FACTS

- Tornadoes can occur at any time of day or night, but most develop between 2:00 and 8:00 p.m. because thunderstorms generally need the heat of the sun to form and tornadoes need thunderstorms.
- Since records started being kept in 1980, 2011 was the most expensive year in terms of damage caused by tornadoes at $28 billion.
- April 27, 2011, holds the record for the most tornadoes on any single day. There were 199.
- On average, Texas has the most tornadoes each year, at 155. Florida has the most tornadoes per 10,000 square miles, followed by Kansas, Maryland, and Illinois. (Texas ranks seventeenth.)

THE CHASERS

Sean Casey, Los Angeles

Every tornado has a different sound. A normal-size tornado going over farmland will sound like you're next to Niagara Falls, with a constant roaring. But when a tornado goes over a town and starts picking things up, it becomes more of a rumble. You're hearing noise from all the debris that's aloft. Then you have these little *sub-vortices,* these powerful little spin-ups that happen quickly, all around you. When one of those little vortices forms, it makes this hissing sound. It's so dang spooky.

The first tornado we ran into with the TIV (Tornado Intercept Vehicle, which Casey created to plant directly in the path of tornadoes) we could see the funnel forming at the base of the storm. Two or three miles to the south, we saw swirls. That circulation was starting to manifest itself on the ground with dust kicking up, but there was no actual condensation tube. We decided to drive for it, thinking it was going to strengthen before we got there, but when we got there, it had actually weakened. Those little dust swirls were gone, and it was like when you're on a boat, and you see

Lubbock, Texas. Tornadoes have created hail as large as 8 inches in diameter, with a weight of nearly two pounds.

the shark's fin, and then it submerges. Suddenly all that reddish-brown Kansas dust just exploded. It went all around us until we were completely blind. You couldn't even see the ground and you could barely see out the window. It was like we were getting sandblasted. The only things visible were the telephone poles next to the road, so we used those to navigate out of there, all while going in reverse. This was a little dirt road so you're not doing a 10-point turn.

There's just nothing like being underneath these supercells. The sky comes alive with violence and beauty and you're immersed in it. You have a visual mountain over you. After all these years, they still seem like they just shouldn't exist. You're witnessing a monster.

HOW TO SPOT A TORNADO

ON RADAR

Doppler sends out microwaves that bounce off objects, reporting reflectivity (the presence of weather) and velocity. The first indicator is a hook echo (pictured). On a reflectivity map, it shows up as a hook-shaped formation at the storm's southeast corner, opening toward the east.

That signifies precipitation wrapped around a column of warm air. The second sign is a velocity couplet. On a velocity map, you'll see winds moving away from the radar adjacent to winds moving toward it. Because radar typically displays away movement with red and toward movement with green, this looks like adjacent red and green coloration—like Christmas lights. When both a hook echo and a velocity couplet appear on radar readouts, it doesn't necessarily mean there will be a tornado, but it does mean it's time to put out a warning. (With thanks to Steven DiMartino at nynjpaweather.com.)

ON LAND

The first sign is thunderheads: puffy cumulus or cumulonimbus clouds. The wall clouds and funnels will form right beneath them, so check there for any organized rotation. Watch the storm base closely and look for persistent lowered areas—the lower they are, the better the chance of a tornado. Another good sign is if the winds are warm and blowing toward that base. Look for any motion or quick changes around a flat, lowered area protruding from the storm base, called a *beaver tail*. Watch the terrain beneath the funnel cloud for any dust or debris that gets kicked up or for rapidly moving cloud laments along the ground. In some storms the lightning and thunder will get close, frequent, and loud for five minutes and then just shut off. That's when the storm gets serious about making a tornado. (With thanks to William Reid, storm chaser.)

HOW TO SURVIVE

THE SAFE PLACE
Kim Cross

Cold fear spiders down the length of my spine every time the siren screams. The wail sounds like a World War II air-raid siren and it means a tornado has touched the ground somewhere inside my county. The weather radio crackles to life, dispatching warnings in a droid-like monotone. On TV the weatherman waves in front of a radar screen blooming with angry spirals.

Sometimes we can see it live, on a SkyCam, a writhing funnel shredding houses and lives as the rest of us look on. When the power dies, that image lingers. The lights wink out and the comforting hum of household things gives way to a terrible silence—a stillness that's absolute.

We grab headlamps and sturdy shoes, in case we have to walk on rubble later. By battery light we pluck our 7-year-old son from the warmth of his bed, gather blankets and soft pillows, and call our dog into the tiny laundry room at the bottom

Washington, Illinois,
November 18, 2013

TYPES OF SHELTER
IN DECREASING ORDER OF EFFECTIVENESS

6
Highway underpass

5
Car

4
Mobile home

3
Ditch

2
Interior room with no windows

1
Basement

of the stairs. We pull a bike helmet over our sleeping boy's head and buckle our own. We get the mattress from his bed, huddle under it in the dark, and wait.

It is as helpless a feeling as I've ever known. A primal fear, knowing danger is close and there's nothing you can do about it. Tornadoes are acute and erratic, leaving one house inexplicably standing between two bare foundations. It doesn't matter who you are or what you've done. The center of your world is asleep in your arms and his fate will be determined by how the wind decides to blow. We could be sucked into the sky and pummeled to death with the bricks of our well-built home. We could be thrown hundreds of feet, impaled by a mailbox, or crushed by falling walls. We could suffocate slowly under a mountain of debris. We could die. Or, worse, some of us could live in a world without the others.

Kim Cross is a writer living in Alabama. Her book, What Stands in a Storm, *chronicles a tragic three-day tornado outbreak in 2011.*

The Demolition Toolbox

BUILDING A SHELTER OR FORTIFYING THE ONE YOU'RE IN TAKES MATERIALS. WHERE DO YOU GET THOSE MATERIALS? FROM EXISTING STRUCTURES. HERE ARE THE TOOLS THAT WILL HELP YOU IN A REMODELING JOB OR AN EMERGENCY.

RIPPING BAR

To remodel, you need a ripping bar. It's got a cat's paw at one end for digging out nails and a V-notch chisel and nail slot at the other. You can do everything with it from lifting shingles to dismantling wall framing.

SAWZALL

There will be a lot to cut: nail-studded framing lumber and cast-iron pipe, shingles, tree branches, even roots. Only one tool handles all that, the mighty reciprocating saw. Our vote is for the famous Milwaukee Super Sawzall.

FRAMING HAMMER

The solid-steel framing hammer is nearly unbreakable. When you're madly tearing out lumber in a confined space or driving a nail somewhere you're sure to hit the handle, you'll be glad you have this puppy.

OSCILLATING MULTITOOL

Although demolition and remodeling can be a savage business, there are times when precision is called for. Enter the oscillating multitool. It cuts in impossible places, making clean slices through wood, metal, and plaster.

SLEDGEHAMMER

No remodeling and demolition kit is complete without a high-quality sledge. Don't waste money on a cheap one that will chip when it strikes concrete. Buy one that's drop-forged and heat-treated. Swing with impunity.

How I Survived a Bear Attack

WHEN A 400-POUND BROWN BEAR CHARGED MY FAMILY,
I KNEW EXACTLY WHAT TO DO: FIGHT BACK.

BY TOBY BURKE

EVEN SUNNY APRIL days can be cold in south-central Alaska, so my family and I bundled up before we went bird-watching. My wife, Laura, and I loaded our three kids—Grace, 11; Damien, eight; and seven-month-old Camille—into the car and we drove about 20 minutes from our home in Kenai to the mouth of the Kasilof River to look for shorebirds. A few minutes in, we spotted an adult brown bear 300 yards down the beach. It had probably just emerged from its winter den. It must have been very hungry.

The bear disappeared behind a dune but for safety's sake we started moving in the other direction. That's when Grace said, "It's right behind us!" Suddenly it was 20 yards away and coming straight at us. "Get together and wave your arms slowly over your head," I said. We wanted to look like a big animal to appear more intimidating. The bear wasn't convinced. It paused then ran right at us. I told everyone to get behind me and not run away, which could have triggered the bear's predation instincts.

Sometimes a bear will bluff-charge but this one kept coming. I held out the tripod of my spotting scope with both hands, like a barrier, and the bear crashed into it. As it pressed its full weight against me, I jammed the scope sideways into its mouth. It swatted the tripod and shattered it into pieces, leaving me holding a jagged stick. Desperate, I jabbed at the bear's face and mouth with the stick but it knocked that away, too. Now weaponless, I raised my left arm in self-defense. The bear bit into it. His crushing force was so intense that I thought it would break my arm. Strangely I didn't feel any pain. I used my free hand to punch at his face again and again. The blows were softened by his thick, coarse fur.

All I could think was that if I went down, the bear would be on my wife and kids—and they'd be easy prey. So I wrestled the bear for what seemed like ages but it was probably less than a minute.

Finally, the bear had enough and ambled off. When it was about 100 yards away, it turned to face us. I thought it was going to charge at us again. That was the most terrifying part of the experience because I didn't have any more fight left in me. Thankfully, it reconsidered and loped away. We called 911 and made our way back to our van while we waited for troopers.

Today, when I think about the experience, I realize we did a lot of things right. But we were also very lucky. I'm a pretty big guy; if I hadn't been as physically strong, I wouldn't have been able to hold off the bear. Because it was cold and I was wearing a thick coat, the bear's bite didn't even break my skin. All I got was a nasty bruise—and a bad scare.

A few days later, we all returned to the same beach and finally got some bird-watching done. This time, though, we were sure to take along a shotgun and some pepper spray.

WHAT HE DID RIGHT
- Didn't panic. Everyone was clearheaded throughout and obeyed his commands.
- Told everyone to group together and wave their arms slowly, so they would appear to be one big animal
- Stood his ground. Most bear charges are usually bluffs and running can trigger an attack.
- Fought back. Black and brown bears usually retreat when victims reciprocate an attack.

Grizzly bears, however, do the opposite, so play dead and avoid confrontation.

WHAT HE DID WRONG
- Went into bear country without a firearm or pepper spray

EXPERT ADVICE:

Nick Meyers

DIRECTOR, MOUNT SHASTA AVALANCHE CENTER, MOUNT SHASTA, CALIFORNIA

A 16-YEAR VETERAN OF THE U.S. FOREST SERVICE, MEYERS HAS BEEN THE LEAD CLIMBING RANGER OF THE MOUNT SHASTA RANGER DISTRICT SINCE 2010.

AVALANCHES

An avalanche needs a few things to happen: a slab—a cohesive mass of snow—and a surface for it to slide down, like a frozen crust, hard old snow, or the ground. It needs a slope of between 30 and 45 degrees. Less isn't steep enough and more will cause the snow to slough off naturally. And it needs a trigger, like a skier or a snowmobile—which is how you get into trouble. If someone gets buried, finding him is no longer the hardest part, thanks to avalanche beacons. Digging him out is. When you've located him, use your avalanche probe: Stick it into the snow as a marker of his position and depth. Take one large step downhill and dig from there. You'll be digging in toward the person—not down onto them.

KEEPING WARM

If you're stuck out in the wild, the first thing you need to do is avoid exposure. Wind saps your body temperature and increases the risk of hypothermia. Keep moving to maintain blood flow and retain body heat. No matter what, never go 100 percent. Always leave a little gas in your tank, because you never know when you'll need it.

GEAR

We use a list called the 10 essentials (below). It's not definitive—I bring a few extra pairs of socks, and in the winter, a hat, a small bivy sack, and a ground pad are also crucial—but these things will buy you time in a survival situation.

THE 10 ESSENTIALS

Map and compass. Make sure you know how to use them. A lot of people substitute GPS. GPS can work very well but it has its limits. In cold weather batteries don't last very long—and if they run out, you're bummin'.

First-aid kit. You want to at least be able to stop bleeding and splint an arm. It doesn't have to be giant since there's not a lot you can do in the field anyway.

Sunglasses and sunscreen. If you are someplace with a lot of snow, like we are, snow blindness is a real concern. And the snow reflects the sun's rays.

Extra food. They may be smushed, old, and beat up, but a couple of Clif bars can keep you going for another 12 to 24 hours.

Headlamp/ flashlight. In every pack. You never know.

Fire starter. There are a lot of options. Try stocking your kit with this: Take lint from the dryer, put it into a paper cup, and pour wax on it. Put it beneath some kindling and light the whole thing.

Multitool. It tends to have a knife on it, so I steer toward that. And it also has other tools.

Extra clothing. Avoid cotton. Once it gets wet, it loses its insulation capabilities and doesn't dry very fast. Synthetic clothing is better. Always have some sort of wind layer. People underestimate the chilling effect of wind. It can be extremely hazardous. On Shasta the wind is just brutal and can lower your core temperature pretty easily.

EXPERT ADVICE:

Nate Becker

DOG MUSHER, EAGLE, ALASKA

AFTER SPENDING HIS TWENTIES AND EARLY THIRTIES AS A FIREFIGHTER AND
PARAMEDIC IN WYOMING AND, LATER, FOR THE NATIONAL PARK SERVICE IN THE
GRAND CANYON, BECKER MOVED TO EAGLE—A TOWN WITH A POPULATION OF 86—
IN 2008 TO LEAD DOG-SLEDDING TRIPS IN THE BACKCOUNTRY WITH BUSH ALASKA
EXPEDITIONS. HERE, HE SHARES HIS SURVIVAL RULES.

GEAR

Always take a sleeping bag. You never know when
you'll get stuck out and have to spend the night or
just need a quick warm-up. And I bring a preas-
sembled emergency pack. Right on top is a pair
of warm mitts in a ziplock bag. History is riddled
with stories of people who didn't survive because
their hands froze. You can walk a thousand miles
on frozen feet, but you can't survive six hours
with frozen hands. Also in my pack are blankets,
hand warmers, a big survival knife, signaling
devices, and fire-starting equipment—you can't
have enough fire starter. One thing I absolutely
won't be without is a Leatherman. I carry two.
And then there's a fur ruff, which lines the hood of
your parka. Even the stiffest wind has a hard time
penetrating a ruff. Just make sure it's real fur.

TRAVEL

The easiest travel is on frozen rivers and creeks
because the land is usually choked with brush and
trees. But remember that the ice is dangerous. You
have to know the difference between good ice and
bad. Clear is bad. You want cloudy. And you want
cracks. Once ice gets thick, the water expands
as it freezes. It has to give somewhere, so the ice
cracks. When you see cracks in cloudy ice, it's
almost always safe.

SETTING UP CAMP

For me the number-one priority is easy water.
You can almost always find enough firewood. But
it takes a lot of time and energy to melt enough
snow into water for 20 dogs. To find the water,
just listen for it. When I get to a spot that looks

like it might have water, I'll put my ear down and listen. If I can hear the water, I can get to it. If I can't hear it—because it's under a few feet of snow and another foot of ice—I move on. If it's a true emergency, don't worry about trying to build the shelters you see in survival books. You would never have time to build most of them. As long as you've got a sleeping bag, the best and the quickest shelter you could make would be to sandwich yourself with your sleeping bag inside a tarp, kinda like a burrito, and then figure out some way to cover yourself with snow for insulation. When it's 60 below and the snow temperature is only minus 20, that 40 degrees makes a difference.

TRAPPING

If you can, set traps every quarter-mile to half-mile. Up here in Alaska, a lot of us catch marten using small leg-hold traps, which are those spring-loaded metal jaws. To set the trap up, first find a 10-foot, small-diameter spruce tree, preferably a dead one. Then tie it to a big tree at a 45-degree angle from the ground. On the end of that pole you hang bait or a lure or both. A lot of times we'll use a visual attractor like a feather or something shiny. Bait can be guts from other animals or even a piece of hide. Once you secure

the trap to the spruce tree just in front of the bait, open it. The idea is to get the marten to climb the pole and step in the trap.

STAYING DRY

Don't work up a sweat. If I find myself exerting a lot of energy, the first things off are my hat and neck gaiter to promote cooling. It is far better to stay a little chilly (knowing I can put clothes back on to warm up) than to let yourself perspire. Moisture lessens the insulating value of your gear, and even the best moisture-wicking fabric in the world won't eliminate sweat. Once you get wet, you stay wet until you get to the cabin or tent at night to dry out.

RESCUE

I always carry high-visibility material in neon orange or green. This comes from my days working on a helicopter crew as a paramedic. It's easy to miss someone from the air, so you want to make yourself as visible as possible. That means movement and contrast. A signal flare works, obviously. But neon material called *flagging* can be tied to a tree. Then, if a pilot flies over, he can see you and which way the wind is blowing. That helps him if he's going to come in and land to get you out.

HOW TO SWIM A LONG DISTANCE IN FREEZING WATER

KIMBERLEY CHAMBERS, OPEN-WATER SWIMMER AND THE SIXTH PERSON TO EVER COMPLETE THE OCEAN'S SEVEN MARATHON CHALLENGE

BREATHE
You must control your breathing and relax—even when the freezing water makes it feel like there's a foot on your chest. Panicking wastes energy.

KEEP MOVING
Even if you think you are not making any progress. As soon as you stop, you lose precious body heat.

FLEX YOUR HANDS
An early sign of hypothermia: claw hands. You can last a long time after this, so flex your fingers closed after each stroke to get blood flowing again.

On the trail Becker prefers to wear gloves under his mittens because "you can take a gloved hand out of a mitt and do something like chop wood or set a trap."

Shelter from the Storm

QUESTION: We regularly experience severe storms where we live, and I want to stock up on emergency supplies. We don't have a basement. Can you give us some tips on storing these items in the garage?

ANSWER: It makes perfect sense to look at your garage as a command center if a natural or man-made disaster strikes. Clean up the clutter and you'll find a no-nonsense space with a concrete floor and great access for equipment. It's perfect for storing tools and supplies.

Your first job will be to build additional shelving and racks to organize your disaster-related materials—construction lumber and plywood work just fine for this purpose. Disasters are difficult to deal with, so you want ready access to your gear rather than having to disentangle what you need from lawn chairs, toys, and sports equipment. Shelving also protects tools and materials from the condensation that forms on many garage floors; this dampness can wreck stored items. If you live somewhere with high summer humidity, consider increasing air circulation by installing a low-speed fan or a power vent in the roof.

Storing fuel for chainsaws, generators, and gas grills brings up an important safety issue. Never store propane in your house, not even in the garage. Find a sheltered place for it outside, such as behind a shed or a woodpile.

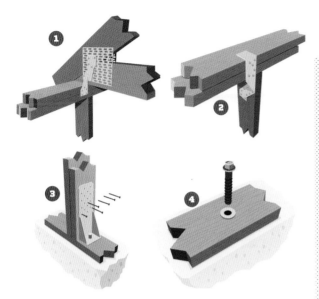

Similarly, keep as little gasoline as possible in the garage. If you have a shed, use that instead. Regardless of where you store your fuel, your safest bet is to use a self-venting metal safety can with a flashback arrestor. A five-gallon can costs $40 to $90 depending on features. A plastic gas can that size typically costs about $20, but spending the extra money for a metal can is worth it. The metal Type 1 can is far tougher, and that's a good thing during an emergency. The last thing you need is to create a disaster of your own with a fuel spill or fire.

Finally, never run a generator in a garage. Even with the door wide open, a generator produces enough carbon monoxide to kill you or make you very sick. Set up the machine well away from the house and connect it to electrical loads with heavy-duty extension cords or a transfer switch wired into the home's service panel. Whatever you do, don't make a double-end extension cord with one end connected to the generator and the other plugged into a wall outlet. Known as *backfeeding,* this sends electricity to every other outlet on the same branch circuit. It's dangerous. If someone forgets to switch off the house's main breaker, the setup can send generated electricity out of the house and onto the grid, endangering utility workers, firefighters, and your neighbors working to clear storm damage.

THE GARAGE FORTRESS

Framing

There are many ways to fortify a garage, from bracing its roof trusses to adding metal brackets ❶ ❷ and straps that tie its parts together. You can even install brackets that better secure the garage to its foundation ❸ ❹. "The most important thing is to create a continuous load path by connecting all parts of the structure from the roof to the foundation," Emory Montague, a structural engineer with Simpson Strong-Tie, says. This reduces the chances of a part blowing off, opening the building to wind forces.

Windows and Doors

The best way to protect these openings is with plywood storm shutters cut to size ahead of time and stored on shelves in the garage. A valuable guide, "Against the Wind: Protecting Your Home From Hurricane Damage," is available at FEMA's website (fema.gov).

Garage Door

Unless you have a garage door rated for high-wind resistance, you need to brace it with a vertical support and horizontal lumber. You can buy a kit consisting of hardware and mounting brackets and a high-strength aluminum pole to install vertically behind the door.

CHECKLIST:

The Definitive Go Bag

LABELED IN ORDER OF PRIORITY, FOR YOUR CONVENIENCE.

First Priority

- Etón FR150 MicroLink AM/FM emergency radio with built-in cellphone charger, hand crank, and solar panel
- Knife
- Maglite LED flashlight; doubles as a weapon
- Extra batteries
- Whistle
- Mirror
- Flint and tinder
- Multitool
- Mylar blanket; lightweight and warm
- Extra pair of weather-appropriate clothes
- Tarp, tube tent, or dropcloth
- Paracord (100 feet); durable and versatile
- Any necessary medication

- First-aid kit
- Nonperishable food, such as MREs or canned goods
- Water bottle with filter, LifeStraw, or canteen
- Canteen cup
- Gloves thick enough but not too thick
- Rain poncho
- Local maps, preferably topographical
- Waterproof matches/ butane lighter
- Potassium iodide/chlorine tablets; a few drops decontaminates your water

Second Priority

- Collapsible shovel for fire pits and latrines
- Metal spork
- Insect repellent

- Toilet paper
- Soap
- Sunscreen
- Garbage bags; good for food storage or a makeshift poncho
- Sunglasses
- Watch; glow-in-the-dark if possible

Third Priority

- Waterproof document packet: ID, passport, birth/ marriage certificates, deed/lease, car title, insurance information
- Cash; small denominations
- 12-hour candle
- Wet wipes (for hot wings)
- Hand-cranked can opener
- Hand sanitizer; bonus: highly flammable

YOU NEED TO FLEE BUT WANT TO TAKE EVERYTHING WITH YOU.

Eddie Bauer's First Ascent Maximus Duffel Bag uses rip-proof and bombproof thermoplastic polyurethane. Closed it's the size of a book bag. Open it has 150 liters of storage.

How to Build an Igloo

NORTHERN INDIGENOUS PEOPLES BUILD IGLOOS WITH FEW TOOLS AND THE
MATERIAL AT HAND. NORBERT E. YANKIELUN, AUTHOR OF *HOW TO BUILD AN IGLOO
AND OTHER SNOW SHELTERS,* WALKS US THROUGH THE PROCESS.

Material

In wind-packed snow, shovel a trench to facilitate cutting the first block. Using a snow knife or snow saw, cut a block 12 inches wide, 24 inches long, and 18 inches deep. Remove the block from the trench and repeat.

Foundation

Mark the center of the igloo with a stick or ski pole, then trace a circle six to 10 feet in diameter. Position blocks along it, using a snow knife to miter the ends for a tight fit.

Construction

Cut a ramp that starts between two blocks and extends halfway around the bottom row. Bevel the tops of the blocks along an imaginary line from the outer edge of the blocks to the igloo's center ❶. Trim snow from the bottom of the blocks in higher rows so they touch only at the corners ❷ and bevel the tops along the angle of sight to the igloo's center. Stagger the blocks.

Exit Strategy

Dig an exit tunnel, ideally beneath a downhill-facing wall.

Last Steps

Slide the top block ❸ sideways through the opening, turn horizontally, and drop into place. Chink gaps between blocks with loose snow. Poke holes for ventilation.

GETTING STARTED IN:

Ice Fishing

JUST BECAUSE IT GOT COLD DOESN'T MEAN THE FISH HAVE LEFT.

BY C. J. CHIVERS

MY DAUGHTER ELIZABETH stood on the frozen surface of a lake near our home, peering intently at the hole at her feet. It was a Saturday during the bitter winter of 2015, and she was holding a remarkably short fishing rod, dangling a metal jig down into the gin-clear water. The jig, spiced with a mealworm, was perhaps 16 feet beneath her, just above the lake's bottom.

Under a roof of ice, this little lure-and-bait combination was darting upward, then uttering and falling, again and again. Elizabeth was trying to entice a fish to strike. I had turned away to scan rows of fish traps when she called out. I looked back to see the little rod bent, Elizabeth cranking on its reel. Soon she hoisted a fine yellow perch into the air. It was perhaps 11 inches long, its bright-orange pectoral fins set against a barred yellow-and-green flank. The fish was plump, bulging with eggs. An eater, all around. Elizabeth set it on the snow beside others. The cold water was yielding its midwinter gems and we would be having a fish fry in our house tonight. There was not another soul in sight.

Our solitude was no surprise. One old joke about ice fishing is that it is a sport many people try once. It's partly rooted in truth, and for good reason: To those who have not been introduced to the particulars of harvesting a frozen lake's bounty, the ice can be a foreboding and impenetrable place. Divining how to bring home fish from water that you can barely see can seem confounding. Where to fish? And how? For what? With what equipment? How do you stay comfortable and safe?

The questions might sound daunting, but most of the answers are simple.

SAFETY

Plunging through weak ice into frigid water (often deep frigid water) is more than miserable. It is a quick way to die.

TESTING THE ICE

Local bait shops will know the conditions but you can double-check ice thickness by piercing it with a chisel or a cordless drill. There are several old-timers' rules out there about ice thickness and safety—two inches will support a man, six inches a snowmobile, 10 inches a pickup truck. I add at least 50 percent to these estimates to account for variations in ice strength and thickness. I started ice fishing around age three or four. Almost a half-century on, you'll not find me on ice thinner than three inches. I feel much more comfortable at four, and late in the year, as ice rots with spring-like weather, I am even more cautious as even thick ice can get soft.

Not all ice is the same. Moving water generally does not form strong ice, if it forms ice at all. For this reason, rivers are generally to be avoided except in protected coves.

SAFETY EQUIPMENT

Some anglers add a host of safety equipment to their kit, including metal cleats for their boots, a life preserver, a whistle, hand spikes, and a rope with knots or a loop at the end attached to a buoy or throw cushion that can be tossed to anyone who falls through. I carry an *ice spud*—a heavy steel bar about four feet long with a tapered blade at its end. When venturing onto new water, I tap this ahead of me on the ice. Firm ice responds with a sharp, solid,

and reassuring noise. Your ear becomes attuned to the sound.

The easiest problem to handle is the problem you foresaw and avoided. If there are any doubts about ice thickness or safety—as there inevitably will be early and late in winter and during long thaws—stay on shore.

COMFORT

You'll need warm clothes in layers, insulated and waterproof boots and gloves, a good hat, and maybe a hood, too. Goggles are a smart investment to protect eyes from glare and stinging snow.

Ice-fishing trips can be as Spartan or as fancy as you wish. My children and I tend toward Spartan and walk out on the ice dragging sleds with the kit and a bucket or cooler of live bait, sometimes adding a backpack or two with a thermos of coffee and food. Others build shanties to live in or roll across the ice on snowmobiles or pickup trucks loaded with equipment, food, and gas grills.

You'll be on your feet all day so be sure your boots are comfortable. And warm. **SOREL's Caribou XT boots** are wind- and waterproof (pictured below). Your feet won't know they've left the living room.

FRABILL

**Frabill
Ice Chisel**

**Kahtoola
MICROspikes**

WHERE TO FISH

Yellow perch, walleye, trout, pike, crappie, sun fish, largemouth bass—these are staples of many ice-fishing trips. If a pond or lake has a healthy number of fish when it's not frozen, it'll have a healthy number when it is. Some lakes are better than others. (Good options include Lake Michigan, Vermont's Lake Champlain, and nearly anything in northern Minnesota.) Local bait-and-tackle shops can steer you, as can other ice fishermen (who are helpful online at iceshanty.com).

The best-known destinations can become crowded and carnival-like, especially at tournaments. (See above. Avoid.) But many other lakes, like the one where Elizabeth hauls perch, are quiet and still, and we usually encounter no one at all as we fish in what amounts to a standard fashion, with some of us setting traps while others move from hole to hole with a jigging rod, looking for fish.

HOW TO FISH

CUTTING HOLES ➡

Forget about casting. Ice-fishing starts with cutting holes. Many holes. To do so requires either a spud or an *auger,* a large drill powered by hand or by a small motor. We use a spud in the early season (for chipping out holes) and a power auger once the ice becomes thick. There are several prominent auger brands, with disputes between adherents that rival Ford–Chevy debates. Just like a drill bit, the auger's diameter determines the width of the hole. Six inches is fine for most fishing, eight-inch augers are popular, and if you're on a lake with huge fish, a 10-inch auger might make sense. But beware: A wider diameter means more work.

Propane Auger (right)

Electric Auger (left)

RODS VS. TRAPS

After the hole is cut, you can fish with a rod or via traps. Rods are used for vertical *jigging,* or lightly bouncing the bait in the water, and dangling live minnows or small grubs. They tend to be short and simple. More than a few old shovel handles or hockey sticks have been repurposed this way. My favorite rod is the handle and piece of a spinning rod we broke by accident about 35 years ago. It works fine.

 HOW TRAPS WORK

Traps, also known as *tilts* or *tip-ups*, are renowned for hooking monster fish. When arrayed along drop-offs or large weed beds where game fish often prowl, traps let ice fishermen cover far more water than they could with a single rod and erase the handicap of not being able to cast. Different waters have different rules for how many traps an angler can put out. Five per person is common.

When a fish takes the bait, its movement spins a spool of line, triggering the release of a small flag, indicating a strike. The angler then runs to the trap, takes up the line with fingers, sets the hook, and plays the fish hand over hand.

Every winter there are days when you are unable to keep all the tip-ups set because you can't find the time, running from flag to flag, to rebait them. These are the trips you remember and the reason you're out there. Once you hit that zone all you need are two more things: a sharp fillet knife and recipes.

STRATEGY: BAIT GUIDE

Successful ice fishing lies in smart bait selection.

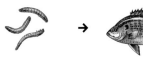

MEALWORMS OR GRUBS → **SUNFISH**

LARGE MINNOWS → **LARGEMOUTH BASS**

SMALL MINNOWS → **PERCH**

LARGE MINNOWS OR PERCH → **PIKE**

TIP!
Saturation comes with costs. The more tip-ups you put out, the more work you face, and not just cutting the holes. Traps must be tended. Holes in the ice freeze on cold days or become buried in drifting snow. You must continually check your line of traps and often change the bait.

The Gourmet Survival Kitchen

THERE'S NO POINT IN STOCKING DELICIOUS FOOD IF YOU CAN'T COOK IT.

BY WYLIE DUFRESNE

I'VE SPENT A lot of time thinking about and preparing for disasters. To tell the truth, I started out on the fringe, buying enough military surplus Meals Ready-to-Eat, or MREs, to put me on a government watch list. But then about a year ago I realized my plan was absurd: My kids won't want dehydrated veggie burgers. During the apocalypse, your duty is to keep up morale—and nothing is better for that than a great meal. To make one, you still need to be able to cook. Here, a few essentials.

FIRE

Matches don't take up much space. Keep them around. And make sure the ones you buy are stormproof. (You can make your own by dipping standard matches in melted wax.) I also recently discovered the Soto Pocket Torch, which turns certain disposable lighters into a minitorch. It's great for mending a frayed piece of paracord or, better yet, making s'mores in your living room.

A CAMP STOVE

One of my favorite portable stoves is the Jetboil Joule Cooking System. I like Jetboils in general, but this one is serious: It puts out 10,000 BTUs, and the pot on top holds more than two liters, which is good for when you need to cook for a few people. You should also have a Power-Pot: The five watts of energy it creates while heating water (up to 1.4 liters) will charge any device that plugs in to a USB port.

A WORST-CASE SCENARIO STOVE

If you are without matches or any other way to produce a flame, you can still make a hot meal if you have the BAROCOOK system. It works the same way MREs do, by generating heat with a chemical reaction. You simply pour water over the heating pack, then put a tray of food on top. So in the middle of the worst, you can just pretend you're at a really weird buffet.

When times
are tough,
nothing lifts
spirits like
gooey s'mores.
And booze.

Shop Notes: Survival Edition

Crayons Can Replace Candles

If you run out of candles, a crayon will burn for up to half an hour, and a piece of cotton string in a can of shortening such as Crisco will burn for much longer— up to 45 days.

Save Your Life with Electronics

The thin wires inside Taptic Engines (the motors that make electronics vibrate) in any phone can be used as sutures.

Laptop chassis are made partially of magnesium. Flake some off with a knife, pulverize it, and add three parts rust to one part laptop. This is thermite, which, once lit with a butane lighter, will burn hot enough to cut through metal and concrete.

Crack open your tablet and prop the metal back casing over a fire. Now you have a griddle.

Start a Fire with Your Smartphone

To start a fire with your smartphone, take out the battery. (If it's an iPhone, break it open. The only other option is to use a pentalobe screwdriver, which you probably don't have.) With gloves on, cut off the ends of the battery with a knife to expose the terminals. Place the knife or steel wool along both terminals to short-circuit the battery, which will create sparks. You can also just stab the battery to expose the lithium to oxygen, creating heat and sparks. In either case, hold over kindling to start a fire.

Purify Water with Regular, Unscented Bleach

Add ¼ teaspoon per gallon of water and let stand for 30 minutes. Then sniff it. If it smells a little like chlorine, it's drinkable. If not, add more bleach and wait 15 more minutes.

Fake AA Batteries

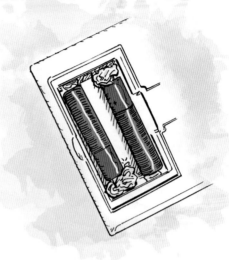

If your flashlight or radio needs AA batteries and you only have AAAs, ball up some aluminum foil and use it to close the gap between the end of the smaller AAA battery and the terminal. AAAs used in place of AAs will die faster, but they'll work.

Homemade Lantern Made of Stored Supplies

Turn a headlamp into a proper lantern by wrapping it around a clear two-gallon milk jug full of water, which bounces the light in all directions.

Use Hidden Water

If your faucets aren't working, what's in the tank of your hot water heater is usable (but you should still boil or bleach it before drinking).

To retrieve it, turn off the power to the hot water heater, whether electric or gas.

Close the tank's supply valve.

Put a bucket under its lower drainage valve.

Open a hot water tap somewhere in the house to let air into the system and water will begin to drain.

When a hiking buddy slid down a rocky cliff in Alaska's Denali National Park, Chris Scruggs spent the next 11 hours searching for help.

TALES OF SURVIVAL:

The Decision

TO HAVE ANY CHANCE OF SAVING
HIS FRIEND, A HIKER HAS TO LEAVE
HIM BEHIND.

JUST HOURS EARLIER they had thought the night in the boulder field worth it. Chris Scruggs and Zach McCutchen had finally crested a ridge in the Alaska Range that they'd nearly killed themselves trying to reach. Mt. McKinley, North America's mightiest peak, was only 30 miles away. The clouds that had dumped rain on them all night cleared. Looking into the valley on the other side of the ridge, they could see glacial melt gathering into streams, streams gathering into rivers, rivers draining the imposing landscape of Denali National Park. The scene was majestic, worthy of their hard work. But then they'd started picking their way down the other side of the ridge. It was a steep slope covered in *talus,* broken shards of rock so loose any step could start a slide. The rangers had said to be careful, choose a good route, and follow it

189

down. Scruggs and McCutchen both had back-packing experience, but not like this, in a place with no trails. They realized they'd have to work together, testing different routes to find terrain they could negotiate. That's what they were doing when McCutchen started to slide. When he came to a stop, he was straddling a triangular ledge of rock just a few feet wide. Below him was a thousand-foot drop. Every other direction was nearly vertical and too loose to climb. He found stability on his perch by turning to face the mountain, but there was nowhere to go. He yelled to Scruggs, who was some hundred feet away, to go get help. If Scruggs were going to hike out, this wasn't the way he wanted to do it. They had no way to exchange gear—McCutchen was too delicately balanced to throw anything, even if they hadn't been so far apart. That left them with only what they'd each had in their packs since the morning: Scruggs had food and the water purifier. McCutchen had everything else: Rope. Shelter. GPS. Maps. Scruggs asked his friend again and again if he was sure: Did he really want Scruggs to leave him there? McCutchen insisted. Looming in the minds of both hikers was the night before, in the boulder field. They'd spent the whole previous day—their second in Denali—trying to reach the ridge. After breakfast and a small lunch, they'd become so focused that they had forgotten to eat again. It grew cold and rainy. They couldn't see through the clouds hovering on the mountainside. They were forced to bed down among boulders the size of small cars, wedging their feet against them to stay in place. Rain got in the tent. Loose rocks crashed down the slope all around them. They'd slept an hour or two, if that. That left them here: hungry, thirsty, and exhausted. After the previ-

Scruggs had no idea whether either of them would make it through another night.

ous night, Scruggs had no idea whether either of them would be able to make it through another. McCutchen had no water, and if he fell asleep, he'd almost certainly fall to his death. Scruggs told his friend that he'd find help that day, that McCutchen wouldn't have to spend the night alone on a cliff. It was eight thirty in the morning. He set off down the mountainside, moving as fast as he could. Scruggs knew that all the rivers flowed north from where he was. The park road ran east to west. He figured when he reached the bottom of the talus slope, he'd follow a river until he hit a bridge. Adrenaline kept him moving. The river was sinuous with heavy brush. He stopped only to take pictures—without a map, he'd need them to direct rangers back to McCutchen. After a while, he fantasized about seeing a bridge around every bend in the river. Finally, he saw it: a man-made oasis. It was 7:30 p.m. He'd hiked for 11 hours straight, covering nearly 20 miles. They'd only managed 10 the day before. Scruggs flagged down a park bus and rangers got word to the Alaska Air National Guard in Anchorage, who dispatched Black Hawk helicopters. By the time the helicopters spotted McCutchen, weather was rolling in and visibility was too low to extract him. They dropped off a mountaineer to help him stay awake until morning, when he could be plucked off the precipice. Once Scruggs learned that his friend had been found, that he had fulfilled his promise, he crashed. In the morning, rangers took him to meet McCutchen as he got off the helicopter. The last time Scruggs had seen McCutchen, he could barely make out his orange backpack cover against the brown mountainside. That was early in the trek, as Scruggs was leaving the first valley. He couldn't keep looking back.

STRATEGY:
HOW TO REMOVE OBJECTS FROM YOUR SKIN

IF THE SITUATION IS SERIOUS, KEEP YOUR COMPOSURE. CALM PEOPLE MAKE BETTER DECISIONS. WHEN YOU'RE TRULY OUT OF YOUR ELEMENT, APPLY PRESSURE AND HOPE THE EMTS DON'T HIT TRAFFIC.

YOU GOT A SPLINTER

Tweezers usually work for big ones. But for the microscopic slivers you feel but don't see, make a paste out of ¼ teaspoon of baking soda and a few drops of water. Apply and cover with a bandage. The baking soda swells your skin and brings the splinter to the surface. After 24 hours, it should be sticking out enough that you can remove it.

YOU WERE BITTEN BY A TICK

Petroleum jelly and nail polish cause ticks to burrow deeper. Burning just makes them release more diseased saliva. Instead, grab your tweezers—the same ones you used to pull out that splinter. Get as close to the tick's mouth as possible, then pull steadily outward so as not to leave any parts in your skin.

YOU WERE IMPALED BY A STICK

Dr. Evan Small, an emergency-medicine specialist, suggests removing the stick unless it hit an artery or pierced your chest or abdomen. (If it did, remove the protruding parts and get to a hospital.) Remove the stick and wash the wound with clean water. There will be a little swelling—that's okay. Apply pressure and get medical attention. Whatever you do, don't use a tourniquet. That starts a clock on your body. You have about an hour before you start causing damage.

5.

Threat: Apocalyptic

HOPE YOU WEREN'T TOO ATTACHED TO SOCIETY,
BECAUSE YOU'RE GOING TO HAVE TO BUILD A NEW ONE.

The Best Escape Vehicles

UNLESS YOU NEED TO GET A LARGE GROUP OF PEOPLE SOMEWHERE SLOWLY, AN SUV IS PROBABLY WORTHLESS IN AN EMERGENCY. THESE VEHICLES WILL SAVE YOU THEN.

BEST FOR A TSUNAMI
Quadski

In front of you: a traffic jam. Behind you: a rapidly approaching wall of death by seawater. You're glad you've got a Quadski, an ATV that can hit 45 mph on either land or water. Retract the wheels, fire up the jet drive, and keep heading inland. Or out to sea.

BEST FOR A BLIZZARD
Diesel 4x4 truck

You want the diesel for range—you can't count on gas stations being open. Some trucks have a Track N Go system, which are like truck snowshoes. Now let's quit this talk of the Donner Party. It just started snowing.

BEST FOR AN ARMED INSURRECTION
Armored vehicle

When the peasants get their pitchforks, flee to your private bunker in comfort and safety. The armor stops common small-arms fire and the underbody is designed to thwart grenades and mines. To the helipad!

BEST FOR AN EARTHQUAKE
Adventure motorcycle

When landslides block the road, you need a bike. Get something with knobby tires and long-travel suspension. If it also has torque management and dual-clutch automatic transmission, your chances of escaping the epicenter get even better.

TALES OF SURVIVAL:

Marooned in the Arctic (with Polar Bears)

IN JULY OF 2015, A RUSSIAN HELICOPTER PILOT HAD NEARLY COMPLETED A RECORD-BREAKING TRIP AROUND THE GLOBE WHEN HE CRASHED INTO THE ICY WATERS OF THE ARCTIC CIRCLE. STUCK ON A SLAB OF ICE SURROUNDED BY POLAR BEARS, WITH ONLY A HANDFUL OF PROTEIN TABLETS, A HALF-LITER OF WATER, AND HIS GPS TRACKERS LOST AT THE BOTTOM OF THE SEA, HE NEVER SHOULD HAVE SURVIVED.

BY JUSTIN NOBEL

MANIFOLD PRESSURE INCREASES. Speed decreases. The helicopter is going down. The pilot switches to autorotation, a safety mode that allows the craft to glide downward. From a height of 3,000 feet, it falls through the fog at a rate of roughly 17 feet per second. But falling where? It isn't until 200 feet above the partially frozen sea, barely enough time to maneuver, that the helicopter pierces the fog.

The pilot aims for an ice floe about the size of a basketball court. In a few seconds he realizes he won't make it, so he expertly tilts the helicopter for safest impact and lands the skids smoothly on the water. The pilot knows the blades could accidentally chop off his head when he climbs out of the craft. By leaning his weight to the left, he tips the helicopter in order to smash the blades to pieces against the sea. This kills the engine, but now, tail-first, the machine starts to sink. Fast.

Freezing water floods the cockpit, wrapping around his naked chest, rushing down the legs of the unzipped survival suit. His gear begins to float—plastic fuel tanks, a small bag of clothes—but the most crucial items are suction-cupped to the windshield: two GPS trackers, one distress beacon, and a satellite phone. Somewhere beneath the seat there is also a deflated life raft containing a survival kit with three flares, a half-liter of water, and a tiny box of protein tablets.

Almost instantly, the pilot is submerged to the neck. There is only time to save one thing: satellite phone, distress beacon, GPS tracker, or life raft. The phone can call for help. The beacon and GPS tracker can give rescuers a chance to actually find him. But none of those do much good if he can't stay afloat.

He reaches under the seat to grab the raft, but it is stuck, and the cockpit is so cramped that he can't get enough leverage to yank it free. He swims out the door, takes a deep breath, then dives back under and into the submerged helicopter. The water is black and salty and cold—35 degrees Fahrenheit. It is difficult to keep his eyes open. But he must find the raft. It has floated out from under the seat and become tangled in the seat belt. He unsnares it, swims to the surface, and greedily gulps air.

Once he catches his breath, he begins swimming to the closest ice floe, the one he tried to land on—160 feet away. The life raft weighs about twenty pounds. The pilot clutches it above his head with one hand and paws at the water with the other. He propels his five-foot-eleven, 176-pound frame, now weighted down by the waterlogged suit, through the waves. Each stroke gets him closer, yet sucks even more water into the suit,

further yanking him down. Killer whales and the elusive Greenland shark hunt these waters, but none of this is on his mind. He is single-minded: Make it to the ice floe.

After three grueling minutes, he does. But this ice is two feet thick, radiant blue, pitted and roughened by at least two years of melting and refreezing. The weight of the suit makes it impossible to hurl his legs over the jagged lip. Yet he keeps trying, searching for the right spot at which to hoist himself up, like a toddler trying to climb out of the deep end of the pool. The sharp ice scrapes away skin. Blood runs down his forearms and into the sea. He finds a smooth section, presses his bare chest flat against the ice, uses his nails as claws, and shimmies atop.

Every inch of him is soaked and his chest is now exposed to the biting wind. He shivers violently, an automatic response intended to generate heat. His shaking hands struggle to peel off the suit, its neoprene material clinging stubbornly to his skin. Once it is off, he flaps the suit up and down, trying to wring out the water. And it is then, fifteen minutes since the belt snapped, as he stands on the ice floe in nothing but his running shoes and underwear, that the situation becomes clear.

Sergey Ananov is trapped on a slab of ice in the Arctic Circle. He has no locator beacon, no phone, and barely any water. The fog will hide him from any rescuers. Night will come. Hypothermia will come. And whatever large, powerful creatures that scratch out their existence in this primordial world—maybe they will come, too.

His eyes wander past the ice and over the roiling open waters of Davis Strait. He is alone, and with each minute that passes he will drift farther from the spot where the helicopter went down, lessening the chance he will ever be found.

THE WORLD HAS BEEN trampled over and clambered up and submarined down, but

if man searches hard enough he can still find a remote and dangerous front on which to battle nature. There are still records to be had. You can still be first at something, the way Hillary and Shackleton and Yeager were and the way Musk and Branson and Bezos want to be. The allure for these men is that simple: the desire to be recorded as the first human to try something and to succeed at it. Immortality. Who doesn't want his name to live forever?

Back on June 13, 2015, the day his Robinson R22 lifted off from the airfield at Shevlino, Russia, about twenty miles from Moscow, the fifty-year-old Ananov was the head of a Moscow trash-and-recycling company. He had already set five world aviation records in the R22 but nothing as ambitious as this: becoming the first person to fly alone around the world in a helicopter weighing less than one metric ton—approximately 2,205 pounds, more than twice the weight of the R22.

According to the Switzerland-based Fédération Aéronautique Internationale, the group that keeps track of world aviation records, there has been only one successful around-the-world solo helicopter flight. But that flight was in a heavier craft and the pilot had support aircraft trailing him, packed with spare parts and extra fuel. The R22 is intended for activities like flight training, mustering livestock, and patrolling pipelines—not circumnavigating the globe. And except for a couple of friends tracking his progress online in the event of an emergency, Ananov was doing it alone. This would be the record to put him among the legends.

He began by crossing Siberia into Alaska, flew south through the western United States, then zigzagged across the American heartland. Since no one had ever achieved such a mad record, there was no time to beat. But Ananov didn't want his trip to look like the leisurely jaunt of a dilettante. He began his days at dawn and often landed in the dark, averaging about 435 miles a flight and sometimes topping 600 miles. He refueled at local and regional airfields. He ate mainly fast food—hamburgers, pizza, KFC—and slept in cheap hotels.

Ananov got to know America, staying the night in outposts like Sidney, Montana, and Guntersville, Alabama. The people were friendly—some of them gave him fuel. The R22 holds about 29 gallons and in two large plastic jerricans kept beside him in the passenger seat—along with his small bag of clothes, chocolate bars, and the occasional leftover hamburger—Ananov could carry another 29 gallons. An electric pump allowed him to transfer this fuel into his main tank as he flew.

He entered Canada near Montreal, traversed remote Quebec, and crossed the Hudson Strait to Iqaluit, capital of the Inuit territory of Nunavut. It was from here that he took off that morning of day 42—less than 3,000 miles from home and certain glory.

Now, stranded and shivering, he allows a few minutes to beat himself up for his mistakes. If only he had dived down into the freezing water once more and retrieved one of the GPS trackers or the distress beacon! If only he had managed to land on the ice floe in the first place! He could somehow have hailed a mechanic to fix the R22 and still captured the record! But none of this matters now. It is wasted energy to even think these thoughts. And so he gets to work.

First he must get the survival suit back on. He can't wring out all the water, and he struggles into the dank neoprene, pulling it up all the way so the built-in cap covers his head. He now has a thick layer between him and the wind, but that layer is soaked, and his body continues to shiver. The suit's mittens have reduced his hands to clumsy paws, and he fumbles with the cord to blow up the life raft. After several yanks, the raft inflates. He takes the cord and ties it to his leg so the raft won't blow away. Using it as a windshield, Ananov lies beneath, flat on his stomach.

This is not the teeth-chattering cold of spending too long on a ski slope. This is the cold of

> **A *third* polar bear walks toward him, sniffing the air, smelling the human body beneath the neoprene suit.**

gangrene and cardiac arrest and brain death. This is the cold of hypothermia. Ananov gets up and tries to walk around his ice island, dragging the raft behind him, but he is quickly panting. Nerve and muscle fibers don't work so well in the cold, as the chemical reactions that enable their functioning slow down drastically. Because of the shivering, his muscles are continuously contracting. There is also the wind—cold and unbearable. He figures the most helpful thing he can do right now is nothing: simply keep as still as possible and try to retain heat and energy. He lies back down under the raft.

ABOUT 3,000 MILES AWAY, in San Francisco, a Russian-American friend of Ananov's named Andrey Kaplin is one of those tracking the journey online. They connected on a Russian web forum for private pilots and first met just weeks ago when Ananov passed through on his journey. Kaplin sees that one of the GPS trackers indicates the helicopter's speed has flatlined. He makes a call to another of their pilot friends in Moscow, Michael Farickh. It is the middle of the night there, but Farickh jumps out of bed and makes the call that counts: to the Joint Rescue Coordination Centre in Halifax, Nova Scotia.

Halifax dispatches two C-130 Hercules aircraft to the pilot's last known position. But it is too late in the day for a thorough search. Halifax also radios the *Pierre Radisson,* a 323-foot Canadian Coast Guard icebreaker commanded by Captain Stéphane Julien. Though here, too, a snag. The vessel is at least a day away, in Frobisher Bay, escorting a freighter into Iqaluit. With no

The ship's crew members
pose with Aranov (seated at center).

other icebreakers in the area, Captain Julien cannot abandon his charge.

But Julien knows how dire the situation is for Ananov. He became fascinated with the Arctic at six years old, watching Super 8 films of polar bears and ice floes with his uncle who sailed with the Canadian Coast Guard in the 1960s. At seventeen, Julien signed up, and by 2003 he was commanding a medium-class icebreaker used for research. From polar scientists and Inuit guides, Julien has learned the Arctic's secrets. He has done twenty-nine Arctic tours, sailed the Northwest Passage seven times, rescued several human beings from an icy death. He decides he will not let the stranded pilot perish. Safely depositing the freighter in Iqaluit, he battles back through the treacherous passage he has just traveled and heads for the Davis Strait.

Ananov knows none of this—and hopes only that the GPS trackers, waterproof to one meter, somehow communicated his desperate situation before sinking 600 feet to the sea bottom. Or that the buoyant distress beacon became unsuctioned from the helicopter's windshield and bobbed to the surface. He also knows nothing of the predator now tracking him. For somewhere in the strait, one of earth's great hunters has stood upright and is waving its head back and forth. It can smell a ringed seal under several feet of snow and a rotting whale carcass from 90 miles away. But this scent? It draws a blank, having never encountered a middle-aged Russian—a 176-pound salami on an ice floe. Moving in its pigeon-toed walk, swinging its front paws out with each step then turning them inward and landing heels first, the polar bear heads off to inspect.

THE SUMMER BEFORE, in nearby Arctic Bay, thirty-one-year-old Adrian Arnauyuma-yuq and his twenty-six-year-old brother-in-law loaded up a snowmobile and ventured out on their annual hunting trip. The first night they set up camp on an ice floe, a few hundred feet from the edge. In the morning, they were wakened by a 1,000-pound polar bear ripping apart their tent. Arnauyumayuq quickly reached for his three-inch hunting knife, stabbed the bear in the face, and then tried to flee the tent. But the bear pounced on him, clawing open his back and gobbling his head.

"I could see inside its mouth," Arnauyumayuq later told the local newspaper *Nunatsiaq News*. "It was all black and smelly." The bear flung Arnauyumayuq aside and went after his brother-in-law, fracturing his collarbone before Arnauyumayuq could grab his rifle and shoot the bear dead.

The Arctic is full of these kinds of stories. They blow around in the wind, drift with the tide. It has always been this way, ever since the Tuniit people arrived five thousand years ago with bows and arrows. Mostly these stories end not in survival but disaster.

Sergey Ananov has no rifle. He has no knife. About four hours after falling out of the sky, he is still on his stomach inside his makeshift tent when he hears the sound of heavy breathing and crunching snow. He peeks out from under the raft and sees the bear, its fur wet and glistening after swimming from floe to floe—a task it can do for days without stopping.

Ananov hides beneath his raft and hopes the monster leaves. It doesn't. The creature bobs its snout up and down, sniffing the air, and lopes straight for him. The bear is about five feet away, so close that Ananov can see the black of its foot-pads and toenails. Biologists will tell you that at this point the bear has one of two motives: hunger or curiosity. Both are bad for the pilot since polar bears often satisfy their curiosity with their teeth.

If I meet the bear face-to-face I will die, Ananov thinks. And that death seems imminent, guaranteed. Then, from somewhere deep in his core, a primeval and spontaneous urge is unleashed. Ananov bolts up, flings off the raft, and rushes the beast—his arms flailing, roaring as loud as he can. And it works! The bear actually gallops away. But Ananov does not stop. He chases the bear to the very edge of the floe with the raft still attached to his leg and bouncing behind him. The bear nimbly launches across to a neighboring slab, then looks back at Ananov, who continues to scream furiously. His eyes are black coals of rage. He is roaring. The bear jogs a bit, sits down on his backside, and looks right at the pilot, examining him mutely. Ananov still roars. But now it is not only directed at the bear. It is directed at the cruel fate that put him here. It is directed at his utter helplessness.

For a full minute, the strange encounter continues. Man roaring, beast watching. Then the bemused bear gets up and trots off into the Arctic fog.

THE EUPHORIA AND ADRENALINE from the encounter with the bear do not last. The hours lumber on, minutes that feel like years. Then the sound of a plane.

> # He does not have the energy to fight off another bear. He has never thought of suicide before.

Ananov cannot see it because of the fog, but with his clumsy mitts he seizes one of the three flares, aims it at the noise, and pulls the cord. A dazzling orange-red flame leaps into the air. Ananov hears the plane arc directly overhead and continue on. The flare burns for 30 seconds then fizzles.

Evening approaches. The cold is deep, raw, gnawing. The temperature is hovering right at the freezing point. Ananov rations his protein tablets, about 2,000 calories' worth, into three-day portions. After that, he figures, he will be dead.

Humans can go without food for more than three weeks—so long as they have water. Ananov has only the half-liter that came with the raft. His shivering is so fierce and constant that it causes him to sweat. He has also been urinating frequently in the survival suit—a liberating release that provides brief moments of warmth and happiness. He is losing water simply from breathing. If all this bodily fluid is not replenished, the corresponding drop in blood pressure will be fatal. It seems a bit of cosmic ridicule: quite literally dying of thirst while surrounded by water and even sitting atop the stuff, yet unable to drink a drop of it. Ingesting saltwater would only speed up the dehydration.

Ananov does not sleep. He listens for bears. He thinks about his wife, Jane, and his children. His twenty-two-year-old daughter, Daria, has just graduated with a degree in journalism from Moscow State University. His twenty-year-old son, Andrey, is studying economics at Moscow State Institute of International Relations. At least they are grown, Ananov thinks. And thanks to the trash business, at least they will be taken care of.

About a hundred miles away, the *Pierre Radisson* finally reaches a section of open water and Captain Julien fires all six engines, 40,000 horsepower in total, plowing forward at the ship's top speed: 19 miles per hour.

IN THE MORNING, another plane. It is still too foggy to see the craft but Ananov, hopeful, lights his second flare. No luck. However, the still-hot flare casing does him some good: He uses it to burn holes in his survival suit at the tip of each foot. Now the urine that has been pooling in the feet and legs of the suit can drain directly onto the ice. The small things that enable man to survive.

Later that same morning, Ananov hears a helicopter. It is at least a few miles away. Ananov knows there is no way the pilot will be able to see the minuscule 12-inch flame. So he decides to save his last flare. The helicopter disappears.

Then another bear. Again Ananov flails, roars, chases the beast, scampers across the ice screaming like a fool. It works again, but without food and sapped by the constant shivering—the only thing keeping his body warm enough to function—he is even more worn-out than the first time.

Morning passes into afternoon. There is a depression in the ice near the floe's edge filled with dazzling aquamarine water. Ananov sets his life raft down, creating a sort of water bed. He lies down and dozes, memories spinning backward, until he hears the familiar crunch of snow.

A third bear walks toward him, sniffing the air with its massive snout, smelling the human body beneath the neoprene fabric, a body that is weakening, ripening. Ananov scares it off in the same manner, staggers back to the raft. He flips it over and crawls beneath.

He does not have the energy to fight off another bear or he tells himself he doesn't. He has never thought of suicide before. But when we humans find ourselves in desperate situations, perspective—our unique ability to view our own situation within the full context of human suffering—has a way of disappearing. Time collapses in on itself. The power to think clearly, the way we would back home, where everything is okay, becomes a vital piece of equipment to be preserved at all costs. Being marooned in the icy brutality of the Arctic has rendered Ananov's mind a gelid mass of fear and uncertainty. He does not want to be devoured and digested by a polar bear. He would rather die on his own terms. As he shivers violently on the ice, he contemplates how he might execute the task.

TWENTY-FIVE HOURS AFTER leaving the freighter, fighting a one-knot current and narrowly avoiding 20-story icebergs and submerged ice hunks called *growlers,* the *Pierre Radisson* chugs into the ice-floe-flecked region of the Davis Strait where Ananov went down. Halifax has drawn up a plan based on Ananov's last beacon point, the wind, and the weather. But the wind is light, and Julien suspects their calculations are off. Instead of beginning the search eight miles from the beacon, as Halifax proposes, he focuses on a two-mile radius.

ALL AVAILABLE HANDS are on deck. The mood is tense. In a few hours it will be dark, making a rescue impossible, leaving Ananov to spend another night on the ice. He might not make it. He already may not have made it—not all of him, anyway. The overnight low could drop below freezing. And that is without the windchill. In such conditions, frostbite can occur in as little as 30 minutes. And even if he does make it, by tomorrow his body will have diverted most of its blood from the brain and other organs to the heart, leading to confusion, lethargy, slurred speech—a revived infancy that will slowly, inevitably fade to black. Loss of consciousness, coma, death.

> **This is not how he wants his name to live on. This is an insufficient immortality.**

Then, miraculously, the fog lifts. And in that moment, as the sun magnificently sets across the Davis Strait, the brutality of the Arctic also evaporates. In that moment, there is no more beautiful and peaceful place on earth.

Captain Julien calls Halifax to convey the suddenly favorable conditions, but their planes are more than 200 miles away in Iqaluit and won't be heading out again until morning. There is one hour of light left. Again acting on a hunch, Julien orders a GC-366 helicopter with two observers into the air. Back on the bridge, a third lieutenant spots a red light on the ice surface.

Julien takes a compass bearing and steers toward the point. The rescue helicopter is notified. They spot the final splinter of light from Ananov's last flare. They spot Ananov. There are no bears on the floe but he is once more running and waving and screaming.

THAT NIGHT ABOARD THE *PIERRE RADISSON,* 36 hours after the R22 hit the ocean, the pilot is fed salad with olive oil and freshly smoked salmon. Everyone wants to shake his hand and take a photo. He obliges, even though this is not anything like the adulation he was looking for. This is not how he wants his name to live on. This is an insufficient immortality.

As he smiles for the camera phones, he is already thinking about the new R22 he will buy. He is already thinking about how he will pack it differently—the emergency equipment, everything within reach. And he is thinking about next summer, when he will once again lift the helicopter into the sky and point it in the direction of the other side of the world.

SOLUTION FROM THE ARCHIVES!

Shirt Washing Machine

"Facing an accumulation of soiled clothing that would have cost at least $10 if done at the laundry," a reader reasoned that his outboard motor could agitate suds. Mounted on a barrel divided by a screen, the rig worked, he claimed—for 10 cents. The clothing's condition afterward was not mentioned.

—September 1926

The Ultimate Survival Pantry

YOU COULD LIVE ON MILITARY MEALS READY TO EAT (MRES) AND CHOCOLATE BARS. OR YOU COULD EAT LIKE A KING.

LAST RESORT FOOD IN ORDER OF DESPERATION

SNACKY
Orange and watermelon rinds
Fiber-rich, pairs well with chocolate

HUNGRY
Tree bark
Remove the tender inner layer and boil strips of it as you would pasta.

FAMISHED
Leather
Avoid dyes, if possible, and boil in water to soften. Can also be roasted into chips.

DYING
Dirt/clay
Dirt is nutrient rich, and clay is filling. If able, bake to kill bacteria, boil for 30 minutes, and strain.

CHECKLIST:

SHOPPING LIST

PROTEINS
☐ Canned ham
☐ Canned salmon
☐ Dried bottarga
☐ Grated Parmesan
☐ Barbecue jerky

BROTHS/ LIQUIDS/ VEGGIES
☐ Really good olive oil
☐ Canned tomatoes
☐ Low-salt vegetable, chicken, and beef broths
☐ Pumpkin purée [for thickening soups]
☐ Evaporated milk
☐ Carrot and tomato juice [to add acidity]
☐ Canned corn
☐ Canned peas

CARBS
☐ Jasmine rice
☐ Canned beans [black, kidney, garbanzo, refried]
☐ Dried beans [mung beans, Rancho Gordo mixed varieties]
☐ Pasta
☐ Bread crumbs

SPICES/ FLAVORS
(In addition to pantry staples)
☐ Curry
☐ Chili seasoning
☐ Canned green chiles
☐ Harissa
☐ Tomato sauce
☐ Salsa
☐ Ketchup
☐ Pastes [tomato, garlic, onion, pesto, chipotle]

Pantry Meals Made With Six Ingredients or Less

PASTA AND PEAS

Pasta

+

Canned Peas

+

Canned Ham

+

Evaporated Milk

+

Parmesan

+

Bread Crumbs

THREE-BEAN CHILI

Canned Beans

+

Vegetable Broth

+

Pumpkin Purée

+

Chili Seasoning

WHITE-BEAN SOUP

Canned Beans

+

Vegetable Broth

+

Canned Ham

+

Rosemary

BARBECUE CORN

Canned Corn

+

Evaporated Milk

+

Green Chiles

+

Barbecue Jerky

Special Forces Survival Tips

BYRON KERNS, FORMER U.S. AIR FORCE; SURVIVAL, EVASION, RESISTANCE, AND ESCAPE (SERE) INSTRUCTOR; AND WILDERNESS DIRECTOR AND CHIEF INSTRUCTOR AT BYRON KERNS SURVIVAL

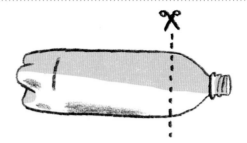

How to Catch Minnows When You're Starving

1. Take a two-liter bottle, remove the cap, and cut off the top quarter.
2. Turn the top upside down and place it in the bottom three-quarters of the bottle.
3. If you have string, make a small hole at the top of both sides and tie an end of the string to each. This is your handle. If you don't have string, use rocks as an anchor.
4. Place bugs or other bait in the bottle bottom to attract fish.

Bugs, Not Berries

Eat bugs instead of berries or plants. The wrong plant could debilitate or kill you. Bugs just taste bad and they're an abundant source of protein. But remember: six legs or less to avoid potential poisoning and roast them if possible to cook away parasites.

How to Make Fire with Gum Wrappers and AA Batteries

1. Fold an open wrapper in half width-wise.
2. Fully cut diagonally from the open side to almost the edge on the folded side. Unfolded, the two ends should be wide triangles and the connecting portion as narrow as possible.
3. Hold the foil side of each end on opposite terminals of the battery. The middle section will burst into flames. Have tinder ready.

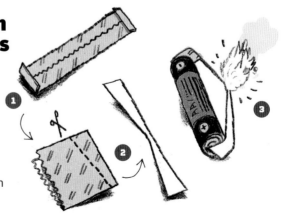

Your Emergency Shelter, Two Ways

TREE WELL

1. Crawl under the biggest evergreen you can find. Get right up to the trunk.
2. Break or cut off enough boughs that you have room to move around or at least sit up without being poked.
3. Use the branches you cut off and any other fallen branches or clusters of pine needles nearby to line the ground for bedding and insulation.
4. If there is snow, use a shovel or your hands to dig it out. Pack down the sides of the hole for walls.

How to Turn Your Car into a Generator

Car electricity runs on direct current, but almost everything else is alternating current. You need an inverter. Some cars have them built in, but you can get one at a store for less than $40. Use clamps to attach the inverter directly to your car battery's terminals. With a 300-watt inverter, you'll have enough amps to run a laptop or even a television.

TARP HOME

1. The materials: a tarp or dropcloth at least 8 x 10 feet and a minimum twenty-five feet of cord (preferably parachute cord).
2. Locate two trees roughly 8 feet apart. Tie your line around one of them. If it's warm, the cord should be higher off the ground to let in more air and vice versa.
3. Secure the tarp to the cord. If your tarp has *grommets* (holes with metal rings), pull the line through them on both sides. If it does not, use a buttoning technique (bottom right, above) before tying the cord to the other tree.
4. Stake your tarp into the ground. If you don't have stakes, use heavy logs to weight the corners.

The Improvised Safe Room

WE'RE NOT SAYING YOU NEED A FULL-ON PANIC ROOM, BUT HAVING A FORTIFIED SPACE IN YOUR HOUSE TO HIDE OUT IN DURING AN EMERGENCY IS NEVER A BAD IDEA. HERE'S HOW TO SECURE AN EXISTING ROOM WITH MINIMAL EFFORT.

CHOOSE YOUR LOCATION

A room that everyone can get to quickly and fit in comfortably is ideal. Try to pick a space that has as few exposed interior walls as possible. If you live alone, a walk-in closet or bathroom is good. For families, a master bedroom works.

CONSIDER THE WINDOW

If your designated safe room is on an upper floor, having at least one window that fully opens is beneficial. A stashed-away escape ladder will allow you to exit if need be.

REINFORCE YOUR DOOR

Interior doors tend to have a hollow core and are easy to kick in. Replace yours with a solid wood door that uses pinned hinges and swings out. The extra resistance from the doorjamb will make it harder to kick in. When ordering the door, request it as a "slab," or nonprehung, and attach the hinges yourself.

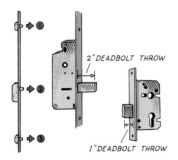

GET A BETTER LOCK

The lock on a typical bedroom door can be opened by a sneeze. Upgrade to a three-point deadbolt with a two-inch throw—that's the metal bar that fits into the jamb.

REINFORCE THE DOORJAMB

It doesn't matter how thick your door is if it can be forced open. Install a strike reinforcement along the jamb. The StrikeMaster II Pro comes with 2 ½-inch wood screws and a built-in strike plate that prevents the frame from shattering when kicked.

How to Barricade Your House from the Inside

When bands of marauders start roaming the streets, how are you going to keep them out? Tear down a few walls and use the lumber and drywall to reinforce your home.

1. Cut your window covers. Pick a bedroom, closet, or hallway partition wall. Use a utility knife or handsaw to cut out window-size slabs of drywall. It's stronger than you think, especially if you double or triple it up.
2. Yank the studs. Inside every wall is a stockpile of lumber you can use to fortify your entry points. Using a hammer, bat, or shovel, knock the studs loose from the bottom plate on the base 2 x 4 and then yank them free from the top.
3. Lock down the entry points. Nail your studs together in lengthwise pairs at a 90-degree angle to form braces. This makes them stronger. Then run three or four braces horizontally across every door, hammering the nails from above and below directly into the frame at a 45-degree angle. If you drive them straight in, they're easier to pop out when somebody kicks the door. Use more braces to secure the drywall over the windows. Try to use longer nails and leave a couple inches of each nailhead sticking out for easy removal.

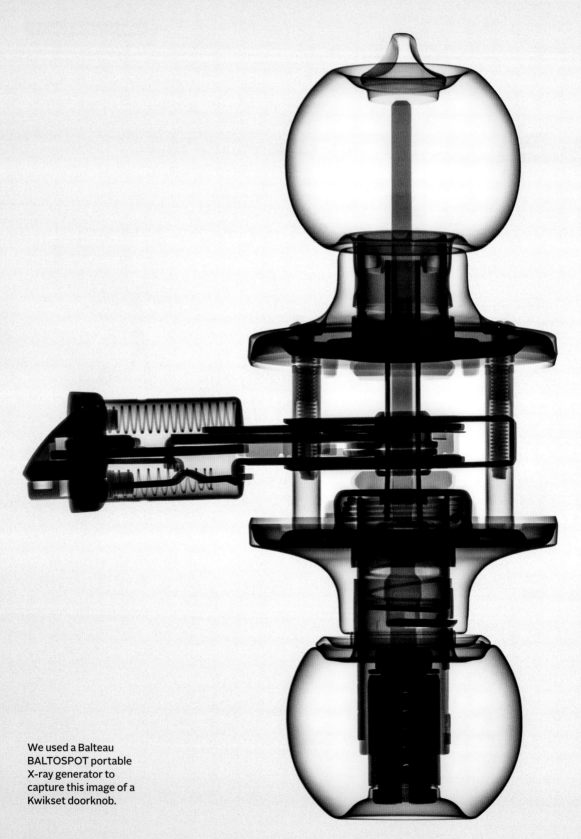

We used a Balteau BALTOSPOT portable X-ray generator to capture this image of a Kwikset doorknob.

Secrets of a Weekend Lock Picker

WE'RE NOT ADVOCATING STEALING, BUT WHEN YOU'RE DESPERATE—AND WHEN THE PERSON WHO HAS THE KEY AND THE ABILITY TO GRANT PERMISSION TO ENTER A LOCKED AREA COULD BE HUNDREDS OF MILES AWAY OR WORSE— YOU'RE GOING TO WANT TO KNOW HOW TO PICK A LOCK

LOCKS ARE DESIGNED to keep honest people out. (Dishonest people can always break a window.) But that doesn't mean that honest people can't enjoy picking them. I've been an amateur lock picker for four decades. I've used a small sheet of plastic or a credit card to open the doors in offices, hotels, and schools. I taught my kids to pick locks, and my young daughter once astounded a locksmith when she opened a tumbler in less than 30 seconds. And I've also helped more than a few desperate neighbors get back into their homes. The more you understand locks, the easier it is to choose the right one for your situation.

FIVE WAYS TO IMMEDIATELY IMPROVE THE SAFETY OF YOUR HOME

1. Buy the right locks. Medeco and Mul-T-Lock tumblers are highly pick- and bump-resistant, thanks to keyways that are engineered with special pins set on different angles. These locks are twice as expensive as other locks, but that's still much cheaper than having a break-in.

2. Use a deadbolt on exterior doors. Otherwise your lock can often be broken by a good kick.

3. Replace hollow core or flimsy glass doors with solid wood and metal doors. If you can break the door, you don't need to worry about picking the lock.

4. Get rid of that "hidden" door key. Burglars know that you have them.

5. Always lock doors and windows, even if you think they're too high for someone to get to. Simple, yes, but often ignored.

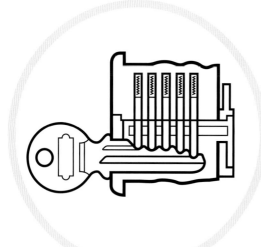

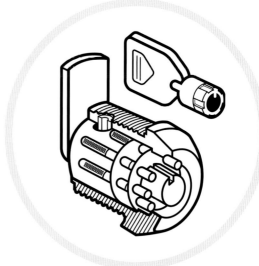

PIN TUMBLER

Used In: Most door locks with a latch or deadbolt

How It Works: When you insert your key in a pin tumbler lock, pins of varying lengths are pushed by springs into the grooves on the key. Only when all the pins are aligned along a particular axis, called the *shear line,* will the key turn.

Vulnerability: Any well-trained lock picker can release pins at the shear line by tapping each pin up with a diamond-pointed pick as he turns the keyway with a tension wrench. You can also use a bump key ground down to the lowest setting, carefully whacked into the keyway. Bumping flings the pins up in the air long enough for the key to twist and catch the pins when they come down, allowing the cylinder's plug to turn.

TUBULAR LOCK

Used In: Vending machines, alarms, bike locks, elevators

How It Works: Tubular locks are similar to pin tumblers. They use cylindrical keys to manipulate a circle of six to eight pins to release the closure. These locks can be more difficult to penetrate because it's difficult to use a common straight-lock pick on a series of pins that are in a circle.

Vulnerability: Cylindrical pick sets exist to bypass these locks. Luckily these tools are not carried by most burglars. However, most people do have a Bic pen, the hollow back of which was unfortunately shown several years ago to serve as an effective pick on a now-discontinued series of Kryptonite bike locks.

WARDED LOCK

Used In: Filing cabinets, some padlocks

How It Works: This ancient lock design is relatively basic. Obstructions, or *wards,* prevent the wrong key from fully turning and opening the lock. Keys for warded locks have slots to bypass the wards that allow the key to freely rotate inside the lock. Generally, warded locks have a latch or spring closure that the correct key engages and opens.

Vulnerability: The right skeleton key, which has most of its teeth ground down to avoid wards, easily fits into the keyway and releases the mechanism.

COMBINATION LOCK

Used In: Padlocks

How It Works: As you spin the dial, three or more parallel discs inside the lock align and a spring latch is released. In theory, attempting to derive the correct three-digit combination on a 40-number padlock can take as many as 64,000 tries.

Vulnerability: By pulling the shackle and twisting through the combinations, experts can feel when one or more of the discs is in the open position, significantly lowering the number of possible combinations. Also, many combination locks have a small flaw in the design of the shackle: Simply twisting a metal shim around and down into the clasp will often cause the lock to release and open.

HEARSTBOOKS

An Imprint of Sterling Publishing Co., Inc.
1166 Avenue of the Americas
New York, NY 10036

ISBN 978-1-61837-272-7

Distributed in Canada by Sterling Publishing
c/o Canadian Manda Group, 664 Annette Street
Toronto, Ontario M6S 2C8, Canada
Distributed in the United Kingdom by GMC Distribution Services
Castle Place, 166 High Street, Lewes, East Sussex BN7 1XU, England
Distributed in Australia by NewSouth Books
45 Beach Street, Coogee, NSW 2034, Australia

For information about custom editions, special sales, and premium and corporate purchases,
please contact Sterling Special Sales at 800-805-5489 or specialsales@sterlingpublishing.com.

Manufactured in China

2 4 6 8 10 9 7 5 3

sterlingpublishing.com
popularmechanics.com

Cover design by David Ter-Avanesyan
Interior design by Zachary Gilyard
Photography credits on page 218